FINDING THE NAME THAT'S RIGHT FOR YOUR BABY IS ONE OF THE MOST IMPORTANT DECISIONS YOU WILL MAKE ABOUT YOUR CHILD'S LIFE.

Whether you haven't yet started to look for a name you really like or you've narrowed the choices down to a few favorites, here is the one book that can help you make that all-important final selection. Among the more than 8,500 names included here, you're bound to find one that's just perfect. And to insure that you have all the facts before you make your choice, you'll find origins, meanings, variants, and nicknames listed for each entry.

All parents want to give their children the best possible start in life, and this, the most complete name guide available, will enable you to do exactly that as you provide your baby with that first, most precious of gifts—a name.

A TREASURY OF BABY NAMES

ALAN BENJAMIN was born in Washington, D.C., but has lived most of his life in New York City. He has been involved in children's literature for almost 30 years as editor, art director, and author.

A
TREASURY
OF
BABY NAMES

by

Alan Benjamin

New Enlarged Edition

A SIGNET BOOK

SIGNET
Published by the Penguin Group
Penguin Books USA Inc., 375 Hudson Street,
New York, New York 10014, U.S.A.
Penguin Books Ltd, 27 Wrights Lane,
London W8 5TZ, England
Penguin Books Australia Ltd, Ringwood,
Victoria, Australia
Penguin Books Canada Ltd, 2801 John Street,
Markham, Ontario, Canada L3R 1B4
Penguin Books (N.Z.) Ltd, 182-190 Wairau Road,
Auckland 10, New Zealand

Penguin Books Ltd, Registered Offices:
Harmondsworth, Middlesex, England

First published by Signet, an imprint of New American Library, a
division of Penguin Books USA Inc.

First printing, February, 1983

First Printing (New Enlarged Edition), January, 1991
10 9 8 7 6 5 4 3 2 1

 REGISTERED TRADEMARK—MARCA REGISTRADA

Printed in the United States of America

For
Lynn Tuckman

INTRODUCTION

The First Gift

Among the first and most important gifts we give our children are their names. As they acquire language, youngsters quickly discover that these names differentiate them from all the others in their growing world, that they identify them as the unique individuals they are.

Along with "mama" and "dada," their names are among the first words they'll learn to say, and almost always the first words they learn to write. And write them they will, almost obsessively in their early years—on book covers, desks, walls, blackboards, and pavements, usually embellished with rich borders and ornaments.

Children are very possessive about their own names and rarely allow anyone to take liberties with them. From a very early age, probably three or four, any variation will be possible only with his or her approval. Once six-year-old Johnny has decided that he should now be called John, he'll fight hard to enforce it, perhaps allowing only Grandma to continue using the diminutive (and then only in private). And eight-year-old Trish, happy with her nickname, will surely balk at anyone's daring to call her Patricia or, heaven forbid, Patty.

The value we place on our names doesn't end with childhood. It remains with us always. And how could it be otherwise? Our names, after all, mark the most important passages of our lives. They appear on our high school diplomas, driver's licenses, and college degrees, and as signatures on our love letters, marriage licenses, and the checks with which we purchase our first homes. They are also the names we pass on to our children and grandchildren, so think well before you decide on that most important gift.

Remember that the baby girl you'll soon be showing off to family and friends will one day be a woman. So before you decide absolutely on Tinkerbelle, try it on for size. "Do you, Tinkerbelle, take this man . . . ?" Aunt Tinkerbelle? Grandma Tinkerbelle? Dr. Tinkerbelle? Maybe you should think again.

Remember too that the baby boy you'll soon be bouncing on your knee will probably tower over you before you know it. I doubt that Marion Morrison would have become the American film hero he did if he hadn't changed the gift of his name for the one we remember him by— John Wayne. Shirley Povich, on the other hand, was able to overcome the considerable odds against him and to become one of the best-known sportswriters of his generation.

But everyone isn't so strong. The Hogg sisters of pre-consciousness-raising Texas died spinsters and recluses, the victims of their given names—Ima, Sheesa and Ura.

Yes, sticks and stones may break your bones, but names may *also* hurt you.

Once the expectant couple has announced its happy news to the world, not only they but family and friends as well begin the search for a name—actually two names, one for either sex. National, religious, and family traditions may play their parts in the final choice, as well as the fads and fashions of the day.

For centuries, many families (especially recently arrived immigrants) chose names for their children which purposely obscured their own national origins—which sounded more "American." Today however, more and more people are finding a new interest and a new pride in their beginnings—their roots.

Where John was once the inevitable form of the Hebrew name Jochannan that Americans chose for their sons, many parents are now choosing one of its variations that reflects these roots—Giovanni, Hans, Ian, Ivan, Jan, Janos, Johann, Juan, or Sean. This volume lists many of these international variations (listed here as var.) as well as variations in spelling, diminutives (listed here as dim.) or nicknames, and definitions. You'll discover, for instance, that John means "God has been gracious."

Black Americans are just beginning to tap the treasury of names from the many countries and languages of the African continent. About a hundred of these names, listing both country and language, are included in this book.

For those who wish their children's names to reflect their religious backgrounds, there are the rich sources of both the Old and New Testaments, the calendar of

3

saints, and the major figures in the history of each religion. Names from all these sources are well represented here.

The tradition of namesakes has always been a way to honor our parents and grandparents, but carried too far can lead to unwieldy populations of Williams and Marys at dinner tables and family gatherings, and endless confusion about just who the letter or phone call is for. In desperation, many will choose nicknames or use their middle names to stand out from the crowd. Some families solve the problem by alternating generations, and naming children only after their grandparents. Jewish children, when not given names from the Old Testament, are traditionally named after deceased relatives only.

Fashion, of course, plays its part in the choosing of a name. Where classrooms today are filled with Jennifers, Ashleys, Jonathans and Matthews, in the 1960s there were the Lindas, Deborahs, Richards and Stephens, and at the turn of the century the Annies, Esthers, Samuels, and Edwards. Some recent studies suggest that children with out-of-date names tend to do less well in school and are generally less well adjusted than their peers. Still, the "good old names" endure, with Mary, Elizabeth, Sarah, Emily, John, David, Timothy, and Robert continuing to appear on lists of the most popular names. See the listings of "America's Most Popular Names," starting page 214.

Where conflicts arise between spouses or families in choosing a name, the best solution is usually the addition of a middle name or, if you're adventurous, the coining of a new name.

4

I hope that the thousands of names included here will make your choice an easier one. However you choose this most important gift, I'm sure you'll do so with care, with common sense and, most of all, with love.

The Twelve Personalities of The Zodiac

ARIES: March 21 through April 20
TAURUS: April 21 through May 21
GEMINI: May 22 through June 21
CANCER: June 22 through July 23
LEO: July 24 through August 23
VIRGO: August 24 through September 23
LIBRA: September 24 through October 23
SCORPIO: October 24 through November 22
SAGITTARIUS: November 23 through December 21
CAPRICORN: December 22 through January 20
AQUARIUS: January 21 through February 19
PISCES: February 20 through March 20

The following chart is only a general guide to the personalities of the twelve signs of the zodiac. It is based merely on the sun signs. If a child is born under the sun sign Pisces, it means that when he or she was born, the sun was shining in that zone of the heavens called Pisces.

6

In a more detailed reading, consideration would also be given to the positions of the moon and planets at the moment of birth. A person born close to the beginning or end of the period governing his own sign usually shares characteristics of the sign adjacent to his own. Thus, a Libra born on September 24, the first day of Libra, would probably share certain of the qualities of Libra's neighbor, Virgo.

	ARIES	TAURUS	GEMINI	CANCER	LEO
Aggressive	X		X		X
Ambitious	X	X			X
Analytical		X	X	X	
Artistic		X		X	X
Cautious		X		X	
Changeable			X	X	
Compassionate				X	X
Complaining	X			X	X
Controlling	X			X	X
Decisive	X	X			X
Deliberate		X		X	X
Dependable		X		X	X
Determined	X	X		X	X
Diplomatic		X	X		
Dutiful		X		X	X
Energetic	X		X		X
Enterprising	X	X		X	X
Extravagant			X		X
Forgiving	X	X			X
Frank	X				X
Friendly	X		X		X
Frugal		X		X	
Fun-Loving			X	X	X
Generous	X		X	X	X
Gregarious	X		X		X
Hard-Working	X	X		X	X

VIRGO	LIBRA	SCORPIO	SAGITTARIUS	CAPRICORN	AQUARIUS	PISCES
		X	X			
X	X	X	X	X		
X	X	X			X	X
	X	X	X	X		X
X	X			X	X	X
	X	X	X		X	X
X			X		X	X
X	X	X				
	X	X		X		
X		X		X		
X	X		X	X	X	X
X				X	X	
X	X	X	X	X	X	
	X			X		
X		X		X	X	X
X	X	X	X	X	X	X
	X		X	X		X
		X	X			X
	X		X		X	X
X	X	X	X		X	
	X	X	X		X	X
X	X	X		X	X	
			X		X	X
	X	X	X			X
	X		X		X	X
X	X	X		X	X	X

	ARIES	TAURUS	GEMINI	CANCER	LEO
Home-Loving		X		X	
Hot-Tempered	X	X		X	X
Humorous		X	X	X	
Idealistic	X		X	X	
Imaginative	X		X	X	
Immodest	X		X		X
Impatient	X		X		X
Impulsive	X		X		
Independent	X	X			X
Intuitive	X			X	
Irritable	X		X	X	X
Loyal	X	X		X	X
Melancholy				X	
Moody			X	X	X
Opinionated	X	X			X
Optimistic	X		X		X
Orderly		X			X
Organized	X		X		X
Patient		X		X	
Perfectionistic	X	X			
Pessimistic		X		X	
Political		X	X		
Possessive	X	X		X	X
Practical	X	X		X	X
Proud	X	X			X
Psychic					

VIRGO	LIBRA	SCORPIO	SAGITTARIUS	CAPRICORN	AQUARIUS	PISCES
	X	X		X		X
		X	X			
		X	X	X	X	X
X	X		X		X	X
	X	X	X		X	X
		X				
X		X	X	X	X	X
			X			
X		X	X	X	X	
		X			X	X
X	X	X				X
X		X	X	X	X	X
		X		X	X	X
	X	X		X	X	X
X		X	X		X	X
	X		X			X
X	X			X	X	
X				X		X
	X					
X		X				
X		X		X	X	
	X	X		X	X	
X		X	X	X		X
		X	X	X		
		X	X	X		
		X			X	X

	ARIES	TAURUS	GEMINI	CANCER	LEO
Reserved		X			
Robust	X	X			
Romantic	X	X	X	X	X
Secretive		X	X	X	
Self-Centered	X		X		X
Self-Confident	X	X			X
Self-Controlled		X			X
Sentimental	X	X		X	X
Solitary		X		X	
Stubborn	X	X		X	
Tactless	X				X
Talkative	X		X	X	X
Trusting	X		X		X
Uncomplaining		X	X		
Undemonstrative		X	X		
Unsentimental			X		

VIRGO	LIBRA	SCORPIO	SAGITTARIUS	CAPRICORN	AQUARIUS	PISCES
X		X		X	X	
	X	X	X	X		
	X	X	X			X
X		X			X	X
X		X	X	X		
	X	X	X	X		
X		X		X	X	
	X		X			X
X				X	X	X
X	X	X		X		
		X	X			
	X		X			
	X		X			
			X	X	X	X
X		X			X	X
X		X		X	X	

Birthstones
And Flowers

January
Birthstone: Garnet
Flower: Carnation

February
Birthstone: Amethyst
Flower: Violet

March
Birthstone: Bloodstone or
aquamarine
Flower: Jonquil

April
Birthstone: Diamond
Flower: Daisy or sweet pea

May
Birthstone: Emerald
Flower: Lily of the
valley

June
Birthstone: Pearl
Flower: Rose

July
Birthstone: Ruby
Flower: Water lily

August
Birthstone: Sardonyx or
peridot
Flower: Gladiolus

September
Birthstone: Sapphire
Flower: Aster

October
Birthstone: Opal
Flower: Cosmos or
calendula

November
Birthstone: Topaz
Flower: Chrysanthemum

December
Birthstone: Turquoise
Flower: Narcissus

Girls

A

ABAYOMI Yoruba/Nigeria: "she who brings joy."

ABIGAIL Hebrew: "source of joy." Var. and dim: Abbey, Abbie, Abby, Gael, Gale, Gayl, Gayle.

ABIMOLA Yoruba/Nigeria: "born to be rich."

ABIONA Yoruba/Nigeria: "born while journeying." Dim: Abbie, Abby, Abi.

ABIRA Hebrew: "strong." Dim: Abbie, Abby, Abi, Bira.

ABRA Hebrew: fem. of *Abraham.*

ACACIA Greek: "thorny." Dim.: Casey, Kacie, Kasey.

ACANTHA Greek: from the plant acanthus.

ADA Teutonic: "joyous; prosperous." Hebrew: "ornament." Var. and dim: Adah, Adda, Addie, Addy, Aida, Eada, Eda.

ADAMA Hebrew: fem. of *Adam.* Var: Adamina.

ADABELLE combination of Ada and Belle, thus "joyous and fair." Var: Adabel.

ADELAIDE Teutonic: "noble; kindly; cheerful."
Var. and dim: Adala, Adalia, Adaline, Adela, Adele,
Adella, Adelle, Adelia, Adelina, Adelind, Adelinda,
Adeline, Della, Delle, Edeline, plus all var. and
dim. of Ada.

ADELE See *Adelaide*.

ADELINE See *Adelaide*.

ADERET Hebrew: "cape." Var: Aderes.

ADINA Hebrew. "graceful; delicate." Var. and dim:
Adena, Adine, Adna, Dena, Dina.

ADOLPHA Teutonic: var. of *Adolph*. Var: Adolfa.

ADONA Greek: fem. of *Adonis*. Var: Adonia.

ADORÉE French: "adored." Var. and dim: Adora,
Adoray, Dori, Dorie, Dory.

ADRIENNE Latin: fem. of *Adrian*. Var. and dim:
Adra, Adrea, Adria, Adriana, Adriane, Adrianna,
Adrianne, Hadria, Hadrianna.

ADUKE Yoruba/Nigeria: "beloved."

AEGEA Greek: fem. of *Aegeus*.

AEOLA Greek: fem. of Aeolus, god of the winds.

AFRA from the continent Africa.

AGATHA Greek: "good; pure; kind." Var. and dim:
Ag, Agathe, Aggie, Aggy.

AGNES Greek: "pure; gentle." Var. and dim: Ag,
Aggie, Agna, Agnella, Agnetta, Annis, Ina, Ines,
Inez, Nessa, Nessi, Nessie, Nessy, Nesta, Neysa,
Ynes, Ynez.

AHAVA Hebrew: "beloved."

AILEEN Gaelic: var. of *Helen*. Var: Aleen, Alene,
Aline, Eileen, Eleen, Elene, Ilene, Iline, Illene.
(Also see *Helen*.)

AIMÉE See *Amy*.

AINA Finnish: "eternal." Dim: Ainie, Annie.

AISHA   the favorite wife of Mohammed. Var: Ayesha.

ALAMEDA   Spanish: "poplar tree."

ALANA   Celtic: fem. of *Alan*. Var. and dim: Alaine, Alanna, Alayne, Alina, Allana, Allene, Allyne, Lana, Lanna, Lane.

ALARICE   Teutonic: fem. of *Alaric*. Var. and dim: Alarica, Alarisa, Alarise, Alarissa.

ALBERTA   Teutonic: fem. of *Albert*. Var. and dim: Albertina, Albertine, Allie, Berta, Bertie, Elberta, Elbertina, Elbertine.

ALCINA   Greek: "strong-willed; persuasive."

ALDA   Teutonic: "rich."

ALDORA   Greek: "winged gift."

ALETHEA   Greek: "truthful; sincere; wholesome." Var. and dim: Aleta, Aletea, Aletha, Aletta, Alita, Alitta, Letha, Lethea, Letta.

ALEXANDRA   Greek: fem. of *Alexander*. Var. and dim: Alex, Alexa, Alexia, Alexina, Alexine, Alexis, Alix, Elexa, Lexia, Lexie, Lexina, Lexine, Sandi, Sandie, Sandra, Sandy, Sasha, Sondra, Zandra.

ALEXIS   See *Alexandra*.

ALFREDA   Teutonic: fem. of *Alfred*. Var: Elfreda, Elfrida.

ALICE   Greek: "truthful one." Var. and dim: Alicea, Alicia, Alisa, Alisha, Alison, Alissa, Allie, Allison, Ally, Allyce, Allys, Alyce, Alys, Alyse, Alyson.

ALIDA   Greek city in Asia Minor. Var. and dim: Aleda, Alita, Alyda, Alyta, Leda, Lida, Lita.

ALIYA   Hebrew: "to go up." Var: Aliyah.

ALIZA   Hebrew: "joyous." Var: Aleeza, Alitza.

ALLEGRA   Italian: "cheerful."

ALLISON   See *Alice*.

ALMA   Spanish: "soul; spirit."

ALMIRA Arabic: "exalted; princess." Var. and dim: Elmira, Mira.

ALONA Hebrew: fem. of *Alon*.

ALOYSIA Teutonic: fem. of *Aloysius*. Var: Lois.

ALPHA Greek: "the first (child)." Var: Alfa.

ALTHEA Greek: "wholesome; healing." Var. and dim: Altheda, Altheta, Thea, Theda, Theta.

ALVA Latin: "fair; blonde."

ALVINA Teutonic: fem. of *Alvin*. Var. and dim: Alvinna, Alvinne, Vina, Vinnie.

ALYSSA from the flower alyssum. Var. and dim: Alisia, Alysa, Lyssa.

AMABEL Latin: "lovable." Var: Amabella, Amabelle.

AMADEA Latin: fem. of *Amadeo*. Var. and dim: Amada, Amadis, Ammada, Mada, Madea, Madia.

AMANDA Latin: "lovable." Dim: Manda, Mandie, Mandy, Mindie, Mindy.

AMARANTH from the flower amaranth. Var: Amaranthe.

AMARIS Hebrew: "God hath promised." Var. and dim: Amara, Amaras, Amari, Mari, Maris.

AMARYLLIS from the flower amaryllis belladonna. Var. and dim: Amarilla, Amarylla, Marilla, Marylla.

AMBER from the jewel amber. Var: Ambera, Ambra.

AMBROSINE Greek: fem. of *Ambrose*. Var. and dim: Ambrosia, Ambrosina, Brosina.

AMELIA Teutonic: "striving; industrious." Var. and dim: Amalea, Amalia, Amalie, Amelie, Amelita, Amilia, Amy, Em, Emelie, Emelina, Emeline, Emelita, Emilia, Emilie, Emily, Emma, Emmaline, Emmeline, Emmie, Emmy.

AMENA Celtic: "honest."

AMINTA   Greek: "protector."

AMITY   Old French: "friendship."

AMORATA   Latin: "beloved." Var. and dim: Amarette, Amora, Amoreta, Amorette, Amorita, Amoritta.

AMY   French: "beloved." Var: Aimée, Amata, Amie.

ANABELLE   combination of Ann and Belle, thus "graceful and beautiful." Var: Anabel, Anabella, Annabel, Annabelle, Annabella.

ANAÏS   after the writer Anaïs Nin; meaning unknown.

ANASTASIA   Greek: fem. of *Anastasius*. Var. and dim: Anasta, Anastasie, Anna, Stacey, Stacia, Stacie, Stacy, Stasia.

ANATOLA   Greek: fem. of *Anatole*. Dim: Anna.

ANCELIN   Latin: "handmaiden." Var. and dim: Ancel, Anceline, Ancelle, Ancillin, Anne, Celin, Celine.

ANDREA   Latin: "womanly;" fem. of *Andrew*. Var. and dim: Andra, Andreana, Andria, Andriana, Andy.

ANDROMEDA   Greek: the wife of Perseus in Greek mythology. Var. and dim: Andromada, Meda.

ANEMONE   Greek: "wind flower."

ANGELA   Greek: "heavenly messenger." Var. and dim: Angel, Angèle, Angelina, Angeline, Angelita, Angie, Angy.

ANGELICA   Latin: from the herb angelica. Var: Angelika, Angelique.

ANITA   see *Anne*.

ANNE   Hebrew: "grace; mercy." Var. and dim: Ana, Anita, Anitra, Ann, Anna, Annetta, Annette, Annice, Annie, Anny, Anya, Channa, Hannah, Nan, Nancy, Nanetta, Nanette, Nanine, Nanon, Nina, Ninette, Ninon, Nita.

ANITRA for the Arab girl in Grieg's *Peer Gynt Suite*; meaning unknown.

ANNELIESE German combination of Anne and Elizabeth, thus "graceful and consecrated to God." Var: Annalisa, Anna-Lisa, Annelisa, Annelise.

ANNETTE see *Anne*.

ANNUNCIATA Latin: "bearer of news." Var: Annunziata, Nunciata.

ANORA combination of Anne and Nora, thus "grace and honor." Var. and dim: Annora, Nora.

ANONA Latin: the Roman goddess of crops. Var: Annona.

ANSELMA Teutonic: fem. of Anselm. Var. and dim: Anselme, Selma, Zelma.

ANTHEA Greek; "flowerlike." Var. and dim: Antha, Thea.

ANTOINETTE see *Antonia*.

ANTONIA Latin: fem. of *Anthony*. Var. and dim: Antoinetta, Antoinette, Antonella, Antonetta, Antonietta, Antonia, Netta, Nettie, Netty, Toinetta, Toinette, Toni, Tonia, Tony.

ANULI Igbo/Nigeria: "joyous."

APHRODITE Greek: the goddess of love; literally "foam."

APOLLINE Greek: fem. of *Apollo*. Var: Apollina.

APRIL Latin: "forthcoming." Var: Aprilla, Avrila.

AQUARIA Latin: from Aquarius, the constellation and zodiacal sign.

ARA Latin: "altar." Var: Aara, Arra.

ARABELLA combination of Ara and Bella, thus "beautiful altar." Var: Arabela, Arabelle.

ARDATH Hebrew: "flowering field." Var. and dim: Arda, Ardatha, Ardatta, Ardeth.

ARDELLA   Latin: "fervent." Var. and dim: Ardelia, Ardelle, Ardene, Ardine, Ardis, Ardith, Ardra.

ARDEN   Anglo-Saxon: "eagle valley." Var: Ardenia.

ARDIS   see *Ardella*.

ARETA   Greek: "virtuous." Var. and dim: Aretta, Arette, Aretina, Retta.

ARETH   anagram of "earth." Var: Aretha.

ARGENTA   Latin: "silvery."

ARIADNE   Greek: "holy one." Var. and dim: Aria, Ariadna, Ariana, Ariane, Arianne.

ARIANNE   see *Ariadne*.

ARIELLA   Hebrew: fem. of *Ariel*. Var: Arielle.

ARLENE   Celtic: "pledge." Var. and dim: Arla, Arleen, Arlena, Arleta, Arletta, Arlette, Arletty, Arlie, Arline, Arlyne, Lena.

ARMILLA   Latin: "bracelet." Var. and dim: Armillia, Mila, Milla, Milly.

ARMINA   Teutonic: "warrior-maid." Var: Armine.

ARNA   Hebrew: "cedar." Var: Arnit.

ARNOLDA   Teutonic: fem. of *Arnold*. Var: Arnalda, Arnoldine.

ARTEMIS   Greek: goddess of the hunt and the moon.

ARVA   Latin: "fertile." Var: Arvia.

ASHA   Swahili/East Africa: "life."

ASHANTI   name of West African tribe. Var: Ashanta.

ASHIRA   Hebrew: "wealthy."

ASHLEY   Old English: "from the ash-tree farm." Var. and dim: Ashleigh, Lee, Leigh. (Also used as a boy's name.)

ASIA   for the continent of Asia.

ASPASIA   Greek: "welcome." Var. and dim: Aspa, Aspia.

ASTRA   Greek: "star." Var: Asta, Aster, Astrea.

ASTRID Teutonic: "divine power." Var. and dim: Astred, Astri.

ATALANTA Greek: a huntress in Greek mythology. Var. and dim: Atalante, Atlanta.

ATALAYA Spanish: "watchtower." Var. and dim: Atalia, Ataliah, Attalie, Atalya, Atalayah, Talia, Talya.

ATARA Hebrew: "crown."

ATHALIA Hebrew: "God is mighty." Var. and dim: Athalla, Athallia, Thalia, plus all var. and dim. of Atalaya.

ATHENA Greek; the goddess of wisdom. Var: Athene.

ATIRA Hebrew: "prayer."

AUDREY Old English: "strength to overcome." Var. and dim: Audra, Audrie, Audry, Audy.

AUGUSTA Latin: fem. of *Augustus*. Var. and dim: Augustina, Augustine, Gusta, Gussie.

AURORA Latin: "dawn." Var: Aurore.

AUTUMN for the season.

AVA Latin: "birdlike."

AVIELLA Hebrew: "God is my father." Var: Aviela.

AVITAL Hebrew: "dew of my father." Var. and dim: Abbie, Abby, Abi, Abital, Avi.

AVIVA Hebrew: "spring." Var. and dim: Avivah, Viva.

AVODA Hebrew: "work."

AYAH Somalia: "bright."

AYALA Hebrew: "gazelle." Dim: Aya.

AZALEA Latin: from the flower azalea. Var. and dim: Azaleah, Zalea, Zaleah.

AZELIA Hebrew: "helped by God." Var. and dim: Azeliah, Zelia, Zeliah.

AZIZA Swahili/East Africa: "beautiful."

AZURA Old French: "sky-blue."

24

B

BAAKO Akan/Ghana: "firstborn."

BABETTE See *Elizabeth*.

BAMBI Italian: "child." Var: Bambina.

BAHATI Swahili/East Africa: "fortunate."

BAPTISTA Latin: "baptized." Var: Battista.

BARBARA Greek: "stranger." Var. and dim: Bab, Babette, Babs, Barba, Barbette, Barbie, Barbra, Barby, Bobbie, Bobby.

BASILA Greek: fem. of *Basil* Var: Basilea, Basilia.

BAT-AMI Hebrew: "daughter of my people."

BATHILDA Teutonic: "battle maid." Var. and dim: Batilda, Thilda, Tilda, Tillie, Tilly.

BATHSHEBA Hebrew: "daughter of the oath." Dim: Sheba.

BATYA Hebrew: "daughter of God."

BEATA Latin: "blessed one." Dim: Ati.

BEATRICE Latin: "she who brings joy." Var. and dim: Bea, Beatrix, Bee, Trixie, Trixy.

BECKY See *Rebecca*.

BELINDA Spanish: combination of Bella, "beautiful," and Linda, "pretty."

BELLE French: "beautiful." Var: Bella, Belva, Belvia.

BENEDICTA Latin: fem of *Benedict*. Var. and dim: Benedetta, Benedikta, Benetta, Benita, Bennie, Benny, Binnie, Binny.

BENIGNA Latin: "kind."

BERDINA Teutonic: "glorious." Var: Berdine.

BERNADETTE French: fem of *Bernard*. Var. and dim: Berna, Bernadina, Bernadine, Bernarda, Bernardina, Bernardine, Berneta, Bernetta, Bernette, Bernina, Bernita.

BERNICE Greek: "she who brings victory." Var. and dim: Berna, Berenice, Bernie, Berny, Bunny.

BERTHA Teutonic: "shining one." Var. and dim: Berta, Berthe, Bertie, Berty.

BERYL from the gem beryl. Var. and dim: Berri, Berrie, Berry, Beryla, Beryle.

BESSY See *Elizabeth*.

BETH See *Bethel*, *Elizabeth*.

BETHANY Biblical place name; home of Lazarus. Var. and dim: Beth, Bethanie.

BETHEL Hebrew: "house of God." Dim: Beth, Betty.

BETHESDA Hebrew: "house of mercy." Var. and dim: Beth, Bethesde, Betta, Thesda.

BETSY See *Elizabeth*.

BETTY See *Bethel*, *Elizabeth*.

BEULAH Hebrew: "she who will marry." Var: Beula.

BEVERLY Old English: "meadow dweller." Var. and dim: Bev, Beverley, Beverlie. (Also used as a boy's name.)

BIANCA Italian: "fair; white."

BINA Hebrew: "understanding."

BINTI Swahili: "daughter."

BIRDIE Modern English, from "bird." Var: Bird, Birdy, Byrde.

BLANCHE Old French; "fair; white." Var: Blanca, Blancha, Blanka.

BLOSSOM Modern English.

BLUMA Middle English: "flowerlike."

BLISS Old English: "gladness." Var: Blisse, Blyss, Blysse.

BLUEBELL flower name.

BLYTHE Old English: "joyful one." Var: Blithe.

BONITA Spanish: "pretty." Dim. Bonnie, Bonny, Nita.

BRANDY for the liquor.

BRENDA Teutonic: "fiery."

BRENNA Gaelic: "raven."

BRETTA Celtic: fem. of *Bret*. Var: Brette.

BRIANA Celtic: fem. of *Brian*. Var: Brianna.

BRIDGET Celtic: "strength." Var. and dim: Bridgid, Bridie, Bridy, Brie, Brietta, Briette, Brigetta, Brigette, Brigida, Brigitte, Brita, Britta.

BRITANNIA Roman name for Great Britain. Var: Britania, Brittania, Brittannia.

BRITTANY for the French region of that name. Dim: Britt, Britta.

BROOKE Old English: fem. of *Brook*.

BRUNELLA Old French: "brown-haired." Var: Brunelle, Brunetta.

BRUNHILDA   Teutonic: "heroine." Var: Brunhilde.
BRYNA   Gaelic: fem. of *Brian*. Var: Brina.
BUENA   Spanish: "good."
BYZANTA   from the ancient city of Byzantium. Var: Byzantia.

C

CALEDONIA the old Latin name for Scotland.

CALIDA Spanish: "ardent." Var: Callida.

CALISTA Greek: "most beautiful." Var. Callista.

CALLA from the African plant, the calla lily.

CALVINA Latin: fem. of *Calvin*. Var. and dim: Calva, Calvinna, Vina, Vinna, Vinnie, Vinny.

CAMBRIA the Latin name for Wales.

CAMELLIA from the flowering plant camellia. Var. and dim: Camelia, Melia, Mellia.

CAMEO Italian: "a carved gem."

CAMILLA Latin: "attendant on the gods." Var. and dim: Cam, Camile, Camille, Millie, Milly.

CAMILLE See *Camilla*.

CANADA after the commonwealth of Canada. Var: Canadia.

CANDACE Greek: "pure, glowing." Var. and dim: Candee, Candice, Candie, Candy.

CANDIDA Latin: "pure; bright." Var: Candide.

CAPRI   for a child born under the sign of Capricorn, or for the island near the Bay of Naples.

CARA   Italian: "beloved." Var. and dim: Carina, Carinna, Carissa, Kara.

CARITA   Latin: "charitable." Var: Caritta, Karita.

CARLA   See *Caroline*.

CARMEL   Hebrew: "God's vineyard." Var. and dim: Carmela, Carmelina, Carmelita, Carmella, Melina, Melita.

CARMEN   Latin: "song." Var. and dim: Carmencita, Carmia, Carmina, Carmine, Carmita.

CAROL   French: "joyous song." Var and dim: Carole, Carolle, Carrie, Caryl, Karel, Karol, Karole, Karyl.

CAROLINE   Teutonic: fem. of *Charles*. Var. and dim: Carla, Carlie, Carlina, Carline, Carola, Carolina, Carolyn, Carly, Charlene, Charline, Charlyne, Karla, Karolina, Karoline, Karolyn, Sharla, Sharleen, Sharlene, Sharline, Sharlyne.

CASEY   Gaelic: "courageous." Var: Casie, Kacie, Kasey. (Also used as a boy's name.)

CASSANDRA   Greek: the Trojan prophetess. Var. and dim: Casandra, Cassandre, Cassie, Sandie, Sandra, Sandy.

CASTA   Latin: "pious."

CATHERINE   Greek: "the pure." Var. and dim: Caitlin, Caitrin, Catalina, Catarina, Caterina, Catharina, Catharine, Catherina, Cathie, Cathleen, Cathlene, Cathline, Cathy, Catriona, Karen, Karin, Karyn, Kassia, Kate, Katerina, Katerine, Katharine, Katherine, Kathie, Kathleen, Kathlene, Kathlin, Kathline, Kathryn, Kathryne, Kathy, Katie, Katinka, Katrina, Katrine, Katya, Kay, Kaye, Kit, Kittie, Kitty, Trina.

CECILIA   Latin: literally "blind," but commemorates St. Cecilia, the patron saint of music. Var. and dim: Cecile, Cecily, Cele, Celia, Celie, Cicely, Cicily, Cis, Cissie, Cissy, Sis, Sisely, Sisile, Sissie, Sissy. (Also see *Sheila*).

CELESTE   Latin: "heavenly." Var. and dim: Celesta, Celestina, Celestine.

CELIA   See *Cecilia*.

CERES   Latin: the Roman goddess of the harvest. Var: Cerelia, Cerellia.

CERISE   French: "cherry."

CHANDA   Sanskrit: one of the names assumed by Sakti, "the great goddess." Var: Chandi, Chandie, Shanda, Shandi, Shandie.

CHANDRA   Sanskrit: "like the moon." Var: Shandra.

CHARITY   Latin: "esteem," by extension, "charity." Var. and dim: Chari, Charis, Charissa, Charry, Cherry.

CHARLOTTE   Teutonic: fem. of *Charles*. Var. and dim: Carlotta, Charla, Charlotta, Charyl, Cheryl, Lola, Lolita, Lotta, Lottie, Lotty, Sharla, Sheri, Sherri, Sherrie, Sherry, Sherrill, Sheryl, and all var. and dim. of Caroline.

CHARMAINE   Latin: "little song." Var: Charmain, Charmayne, Charmian, Charmion, Charmione, Sharmayne.

CHAUSIKU   Swahili/East Africa: "born at night."

CHAVA   Hebrew: "life-giving." Var: Chavva, Chaya.

CHAYA   Hebrew: fem. of *Chaim*.

CHELSEA   for the place name in London or New York.

CHERIE   French: "dear one." Var: Cher, Chere.

CHERYL   See *Charlotte*.

CHIQUITA Spanish: "little one."

CHLOE Greek: "blooming." Var: Cloe.

CHLORIS Greek: the goddess of flowers. Var. and dim: Chloras, Chlorie, Chlorisse, Lori, Loris.

CHRISTABELLE combination of Christine and Belle, thus "beautiful Christian."

CHRISTINE Greek: fem. of *Christian*. Var. and dim: Chris, Chrissie, Chrissy, Christa, Christiana, Christiane, Christie, Christin, Christina, Crista, Cristin, Cristina, Cristine, Kirsten, Kirstin, Kris, Krista, Kristiana, Kristiane, Kristin, Kristina, Kristine, Teena, Tina.

CICELY from a Roman clan name. Var: Ciceley, Cicelie, Cicily, Cicly. (Also see *Cecilia*.)

CINDERELLA French: from the fairy tale "Cinderella." Dim: Cindie, Cindy.

CLAIR, CLARE See *Clara*.

CLARA Latin: "bright; shining." Var. and dim: Claire, Clare, Claretta, Clarette, Clarine, Clarita, Klara, Klare. (Also used as a fem. of *Clarence*.)

CLARABELLE combination of Clara and Belle, thus "bright and beautiful." Var: Clarabel, Clarabella, Claribel, Claribelle.

CLARISSA Latin: "made famous." Var: Clarice, Claris, Clarisa, Clarise, Clarisse.

CLAUDIA Latin: fem. of *Claudius*. Var. and dim: Claude, Claudette, Claudina, Claudine.

CLELIA Latin: a legendary Roman heroine.

CLEMATIA Greek: "vine."

CLEMENTINE Latin: fem. of *Clement*. Var. and dim: Clem, Clemence, Clementia, Clementina, Klementine.

CLEOPATRA Greek: "of a famous father." Dim: Cleo.

CLORINDA a name coined by the Italian poet Tasso. Var: Clorinde.

CLOTHILDA Teutonic: "battle maid." Var: Clothilde, Clotilda, Clotilde.

CLOVER from the flower clover.

CLYTIE Greek: "splendid." Var: Clyte.

COLETTE Latin: "victorious." Var: Coletta, Collette.

COLLEEN Gaelic: "maiden." Var: Coleen, Colene, Collene.

COLUMBA Latin: "dove." Var. and dim: Collie, Colly, Colomba, Colombe, Colombia, Columbia, Columbina, Columbine.

COMFORT French: "aid; comfort."

CONCEPTION Latin: "beginning." Var. and dim: Concepcion, Concha, Conchita.

CONCORDIA Latin: "harmony." Var. Concorde.

CONSOLATA Italian: "consolation."

CONSTANCE Latin: "constancy." Var. and dim: Connie, Conny, Constancy, Constanta, Constantia, Constantina, Constanza, Konstanza.

CONSUELA Spanish: "consolation." Var: Consuelo.

CORA Greek: "maiden." Var. and dim: Corene, Coretta, Corette, Corina, Corinna, Corinne, Corissa, Corita, Coritta, Corrie, Corrina, Cory, Kora.

CORABELLE combination of Cora and Belle, thus "beautiful maiden."

CORAL Latin: "sea coral." Var: Coralie, Coralina, Coraline, Corella.

CORDELIA Celtic: "jewel of the sea." Var. and dim: Cordella, Cordellia, Delia, Della.

CORETTA See *Cora*.

CORINNE See *Cora*.

CORINTHIA from the Greek city of Corinth.

CORLISS Celtic: "good-natured."

CORNELIA Latin: fem. of *Cornelius*. Var. and dim: Cornela, Cornella, Cornelle, Nela, Nelia, Nella, Nellie, Nelly.

COSIMA Greek: fem. of *Cosmo*. Var: Cosma.

CRESSIDA Greek: "golden." Var: Cresida, Cressa.

CRISPINA Latin: fem. of *Crispin*. Var. and dim: Crispa, Krispa, Krispin, Krispina.

CRYSTAL Latin: "brilliant; pure." Var: Chrystal, Kristal, Kristol, Krystal, Krystol.

CYNARA Greek: perhaps from the Aegean island of Zinara. Var: Zinara.

CYNTHIA Greek: the goddess of the moon. Dim: Cindy, Cynthie.

CYPRIA Greek: from the island of Cyprus. Var: Cipria, Cipriana, Cypra, Cypriana.

CYRA Greek: fem. of *Cyrus*. Var: Kira.

CYRENA Greek: the water nymph. Var: Cyra.

CYRILLA Latin: fem. of *Cyril*. Var: Cirila, Cirilla.

CYTHEREA Greek: a title assigned to Venus, from the island of Cythera, her supposed birthplace. Var: Cytheria.

D

DACIA Latin: from the Roman province of Dacia. Var: Dachia.

DAFFODIL Greek: from the flower daffodil. Var: Dafodil.

DAFNA Hebrew: "laurel."

DAGMAR Danish: "joy of the Danes." Var. and dim: Dagmara, Mara.

DAGNA Teutonic: "fair day." Var: Dagnah.

DAHLIA Latin: from the flower dahlia. Var: Dalia, Dallia.

DAHOMA from the African republic of Dahomey. Var: Dahomey, Dahomie.

DAISY Old English: "eye of the day." Var: Daisie.

DALE Teutonic: "valley dweller." Var: Dail, Daile, Dayle. (Also used as a boy's name.)

DALIA Hebrew: "branch." Var: Dalit.

DALILA Swahili/East Africa: "gentle." Var: Dalia.

DALLAS for the city in Texas. (Also used as a boy's name.)

DAMALIS Greek: "conqueror." Var: Damala, Damalas, Damali, Damalla.

DAMARA Greek: "gentle." Var. and dim: Damaris, Damarra, Mara.

DAMITA Spanish: "young lady."

DANA See *Daniela*.

DANICA Slavic: "morning star."

DANIELA Hebrew: fem. of *Daniel*. Var. and dim: Dana, Danella, Danelle, Daniella, Danielle, Danila, Danilla, Danita, Daniva, Danya.

DAPHNE Greek: "laurel tree." Var: Daffney, Daphna, Daphney.

DARA Hebrew: "house of wisdom." Var: Dahra, Darra.

DARCIE Old French: "from the fortress." Var: Darcey, Darcia, Darcy.

DARDA Hebrew: "pearl of wisdom." Var: Dardia.

DARDANELLA from the Dardanelles, the straits separating Europe and Asia.

DARICE Greek: fem. of *Darius*. Var. and dim: Dari, Daria, Darise, Darrice.

DARLENE Old French: "dear one." Var. and dim: Darla, Darleen, Darline, Darlyne, Daryl, Daryle.

DAVIDA Hebrew: fem. of *David*. Var: Daveta, Davina, Davita, Vida.

DAWN Anglo-Saxon: "break of day." Var: Dawne.

DEANA Old English: fem. of *Dean*. Var: Deanna.

DEBORAH Hebrew: "the bee." Var. and dim: Debbie, Debby, Debora, Debra, Devora, Devorah.

DECEMBRA from the month December.

DECIMA Latin: "the tenth (child)."

DEIRDRE Gaelic: "sorrow." Dim: Dee, Deedee.

DELIA Greek: a title for Artemis, the moon goddess, supposedly born on the island of Delos.

DELICIA Latin: "delightful."

DELILAH Hebrew: "brooding." Var. and dim: Dalila, Delila, Lila.

DELMARA Spanish: "from the sea." Var: Delma.

DELPHINE Greek: from the flower delphinium. Var: Delfina, Delfine, Delfinia, Delphina, Delphinia.

DEMETRIA Greek: from Demeter, goddess of fertility. Var: Demetra, Demitria, Dimitra, Dimitria.

DENISE Greek: fem. of *Dennis*. Var: Denice, Denyce, Denyse.

DERORA Hebrew: "freedom." Var: Derorah, Derorice, Derorit, Drora.

DESIRÉE French: "longed for." Var: Desirea.

DESMA Greek: "vow; pledge."

DEVI Sanskrit: one of the names of the Hindu goddess Sakti. Var: Deva.

DEVONA English: from Devon or Devonshire. Var: Devonna.

DIAMANTA French: "like a diamond." Var: Diama, Diamante, Diamond.

DIANA Latin: the Roman goddess of the moon and the hunt. Var. and dim: Deana, Deanna, Diane, Dianna, Dianne, Dyana, Dyane, Dyanna, Dyanne.

DIANE See *Diana*.

DIANTHA Greek: from the flower dianthus. Var: Dianthe, Dianthia.

DIDO Greek: the legendary queen of Carthage.

DILYS Welsh: fem. of *Dylan*. Var: Dylana.

DINAH Hebrew: "the judged." Var: Deena, Dina.

DIONE Greek: the mother of Aphrodite. Var: Diona, Dionis, Dionna, Dionne.

DIXIE American English: "girl of the South."

DIZA Hebrew: "joy." Var: Ditza, Ditzah.

DOCILLA Latin: "gentle; teachable." Var: Docila.

DODI Hebrew: "beloved." Var: Doda, Dodie.

DOE Anglo-Saxon: "deer."

DOLLY See *Dorothy*.

DOLORES Spanish: "sorrows." Var. and dim: Delora, Delores, Deloris, Dolly, Doloria, Dolorita, Lola, Lolita, Lolly.

DOMINICA Latin: "the Lord's." Var: Domenica, Dominga, Dominique.

DONALDA Scotch: fem. of *Donald*. Var: Donella.

DONATA Latin: "gift." Var: Donia.

DONNA Latin: "lady."

DORA Greek: "gift." Var. and dim: Doralin, Doralynne, Doreen, Dorelia, Dorena, Doretta, Dorette, Dori, Dorita, Dorrie. (Also a variation of *Dorothy*.)

DORCAS Greek: "gazelle." Var: Dorca, Dorcea, Dorcia.

DORÉ French: "golden." Var: Dorée, Doreen, Dorene.

DORINDA Greek: "beautiful gift."

DORIS Greek: "of the sea." Var: Dorea, Doria, Dorice, Dorise, Dorisse, Dorris, Dorrise.

DOROTHY Greek: "gift of God." Var. and dim: Doll, Dollie, Dolly, Dorotea, Dorothea, Dorothie, Dorthea, Dorthy, Dot, Dottie, Dotty, and all variations and diminutives of Dora.

DORYA Hebrew: "God's generation."

DOVA Hebrew: fem. of *Dov*. Var: Doveva, Dovit.

DOVE Old English: "dove."

DRUSILLA Greek: "soft-eyed." Var. and dim: Dru, Drucie, Drucilla, Drusa, Drusie, Drusille.

DULCIE Latin: "sweet." Var. and dim: Dulcea, Dulcia, Dulcina, Dulcine, Dulcy.

E

EARLENE   Old English: "noblewoman." Var: Earline, Erlene, Erline.

EARTHA   Old English: "the earth." Var: Erda, Ertha, Herta, Hertha. (Also see *Areth*.)

EASTER   from the holiday Easter.

EBONY   from the black wood of India and Ceylon. Var: Ebonie.

ECHO   Greek: the nymph who loved Narcissus.

EDANA   Gaelic: "fiery one."

EDEN   Hebrew: "delight." (Also used as a boy's name.)

EDITH   Teutonic: "rich gift." Var. and dim: Eadie, Eda, Edie, Edita, Edite, Editha, Edithe, Edyth, Edythe, Eydie.

EDLYN   Old English: "noble one." Var: Edla, Edlynne.

EDMUNDA   Old English: fem. of *Edmund*. Var. and dim: Eddie, Eddy, Edmée, Edmonda.

EDNA Hebrew: "rejuvenation." Var. and dim: Eddie, Eddy, Ednah.

EDRA Hebrew: "powerful." Var. and dim: Eddie, Eddra, Eddy, Edrea, Edris.

EDWARDA Old English: fem. of *Edward*. Var. and dim: Eddie, Eddy, Edwardina, Edwardine.

EDWINA Old English: fem. of *Edwin*. Var. and dim: Eadwina, Eadwine, Eddie, Eddy, Edina, Edine, Edwine, Edwinna, Winnie, Winny.

EFRONA Hebrew: fem. of *Efron*.

EGBERTA Old English: fem. of *Egbert*. Var. and dim: Berta, Bertie, Egbertina, Egbertine.

EGLANTINE Old French: "wild rose." Var: Eglantina.

EILEEN See *Aileen*.

ELAINE See *Helen*.

ELBA for the island off the coast of Italy.

ELDRIDA Anglo-Saxon: "wise counselor." Var: Eldreda.

ELEANORE See *Helen*.

ELECTRA Greek: "shining one."

ELIANA Hebrew: "God's answer." Dim: Ellie.

ELIORA Hebrew: "God is my light." Dim: Ellie.

ELIZABETH Hebrew: "consecrated to God." Var. and dim: Babette, Babs, Bess, Bessie, Bessy, Beth, Betsey, Betsy, Betta, Bette, Bettie, Bettina, Betty, Elisa, Elisabeth, Elisabetta, Elise, Elissa, Eliza, Elsa, Elsabet, Elsbeth, Else, Elsie, Elspeth, Elyse, Libby, Lisa, Lisabetta, Lisbeth, Lise, Lisetta, Lisette, Liza, Lizabeth, Lizabetta, Lizetta, Lizette, Lizzie, Lizzy.

ELLA See *Helen*.

ELLEN See *Helen*.

ELLICE Greek: fem. of *Elias* or *Ellis*. Var: Ellise.

ELMA Greek: fem. of *Elmo*.

ELOISE See *Louise*.

ELSA, ELSIE See *Elizabeth*.

ELVIRA Spanish: "elfin." Var. and dim: Alvira, Elva, Elvia, Elvina.

ELVISA Old Norse: fem. of *Elvis*.

EMERALD from the gem emerald. Var. and dim: Emeraude, Esme, Esmeralda.

EMILY See *Amelia*.

EMINA Latin: "distinguished."

EMMANUELA Hebrew: fem. of *Emmanuel*. Var: Emanuela, Mannuela, Manuela, Manuella.

EMUNA Hebrew: "faith." Var. and dim: Emmie, Emunah.

ENAM Ewe/Ghana: "God's gift."

ENDORA Hebrew: "fountain."

ENID Celtic: "pure."

ENRICA Italian: fem. of *Enrico* or *Henry*. Var: Enrika.

ERICA Teutonic: fem. of *Eric*. Var. and dim: Erika, Rickie, Ricky.

ERINA Gaelic: "from Ireland." Var: Erin, Erinne.

ERMA Teutonic: "strong." Var: Ermina, Ermine, Erminia, Erminie, Hermina, Hermine, Herminia, Herminie, Hermione, Irma, Irme, Irmina, Irmine.

ERNESTINE Teutonic: fem. of *Ernest*. Var. and dim: Erna, Ernesta, Ernestina, Teena, Tina.

ESTELLE Latin: "star." Var. and dim: Essie, Estella, Estrella, Estrellita, Stella.

ESTHER Hebrew, Persian: "star." Var. and dim: Essa, Essie, Esta, Ester, Etta, Ettie, Etty, Hester, Hesther, Hetty.

ETHEL Teutonic: "noble." Var: Ethelda, Etheline, Ethelyn, Ethelynne, Ethyl.

ETTA See *Esther*.

EUDOCIA Greek: "respected." Var. and dim: Doxie, Doxy, Eudosia, Eudoxia.

EUDORA Greek: "generous gift." Dim: Dora, Euda.

EUGENIA Greek: "wellborn." Var. and dim: Eugenie, Gena, Gina, Ginny, Jennie, Jenny.

EULALIA Greek: "fair of speech." Var. and dim: Eula, Eulalie.

EUNICE Greek: "joyful; victorious."

EUPHEMIA Greek: "of good reputation." Var. and dim: Effie, Eufemia, Euphemie.

EUPHRATA from the river Euphrates.

EUROPA Greek: from the continent of Europe.

EURYDICE Greek: the wife of Orpheus.

EUSTACIA Latin: fem. of *Eustace*. Var. and dim: Eustasia, Stacey, Stacie, Stasia.

EUXINA from the Euxine, or Black, Sea.

EVADNE Greek: "fortunate." Var: Evadna.

EVANGELINE Greek: "bearer of good news." Var. and dim: Eva, Evangela, Eve.

EVE Hebrew: "life-giving." Var. and dim: Eba, Ebba, Eva, Evalina, Evelina, Eveline, Evelyn, Evelyne, Evelynne, Evita, Evlyn, Evlyne, Evlynne.

EVELYN See *Eve*.

EZARA Hebrew: fem. of *Ezra*. Var: Ezraela, Ezrela, Ezrella.

F

FABIANA Latin: fem. of *Fabian*. Var: Fabia.

FAITH English: "belief; loyalty." Var: Fae, Fay, Faye.

FANCHON French: dim. of *Frances*. Var. and dim: Fanchette, Fanny.

FANCY Middle English: "imagination." Var. and dim: Fancie, Fanny.

FANNY See *Frances*.

FANYA Slavic: "free." Var. and dim: Fania, Fanny.

FATIMA Arabic: the favorite daughter of Mohammed. Var: Fatimah, Fatma, Fatmah.

FAUSTINE Latin: fem. of *Faust*. Var. and dim: Fausta, Faustina.

FAWN Old French: "young deer." Var. and dim: Faun, Fauna, Faunia, Fawna, Fawnia.

FAY Old French: "fairy." Var: Fae, Faye, Fayetee, Fayina. (Also see *Faith*.)

FAYANNE   Combination of *Fay* and *Anne*. Var: Fayanna.

FAYOLA   Yoruba/Nigeria: "lucky."

FELDA   Teutonic: "field."

FELICIA   Latin: "happy." Var: Felice, Felicidad, Felicie, Felicity, Felise.

FENELLA   Celtic: "white-shouldered." Var: Finella.

FERN   Greek: "feather." Var: Ferna, Ferne.

FERNANDA   Teutonic: fem. of Ferdinand. Var: Ferdinanda, Ferdinande.

FIDELITY   Latin: "faithfulness." Var: Fidela, Fidelia, Fidella, Fidelle, Fidellia.

FIFI   See *Josephine*.

FIONA   Celtic: "fair-skinned." Var: Fionna, Fionne, Phionna, Viona, Vionna.

FLAVIA   Latin: "yellow-haired."

FLETA   Old English: "swift." Var: Fleda.

FLEUR   French: "flower." Dim: Fleurette, Flora. (Also see *Florence*.)

FLORA   See *Florence*.

FLORENCE   Latin: "flowering." Var. and dim: Fiora, Fiorenza, Flo, Flora, Florance, Florencia, Floria, Florida, Florinda, Florinde, Florine, Floris, Florisse, Flossie, Flossy.

FLORIDA   for the American state.

FLOSSIE   See Florence.

FLOWER   English: "bloom." (Also see *Fleur; Florence*.)

FOLA   Yoruba/Nigeria: "honorable."

FONDA   Latin: "foundation."

FORTUNE   Latin: "destiny." Var: Fortuna.

FRANCES   Latin: fem. of *Francis*. Var. and dim: Fan, Fancy, Fania, Fannie, Fanny, Fanya, Fran, Francesca, Francie, Francina, Francine, Françoise,

Francyne, Frankie, Franky, Frannie, Franny. (Also see *Fanchon*.)

FREDERICA Teutonic: fem. of *Frederick*. Var. and dim: Federica, Freda, Fredda, Freddy, Frederika, Frederique, Fredrika, Frida, Frieda, Rica, Ricca, Ricki, Rickie, Ricky, Rikki.

FREYA Norse: the goddess of fruitfulness.

FRIEDA See *Frederica*.

FRITZIE Teutonic: fem. of *Fritz*. Var: Fritzi, Fritzy.

FRONDE Latin: "leafy branch." Var: Fronda.

FULVIA Latin: "golden-haired."

G

GABRIELLE Hebrew: fem. of *Gabriel*. Var. and dim: Gabriela, Gabriella, Gaby. (Also see *Gavrila*.)

GAIA Greek: an earth goddess.

GAIL, GALE See *Abigail*.

GALATEA Greek: "ivory-colored."

GALI Hebrew: "fountain." Var: Galice, Galit.

GALILEA from the province of Galilee. Var: Galileah.

GALINA Russian: var. of *Helen*.

GALYA Hebrew: "God has redeemed."

GAMMA Greek: "the third (child)."

GANIT Hebrew: "garden." Var: Gana, Ganice.

GARDA Teutonic: "protected." Var: Gerda.

GARDENIA from the flower gardenia. Var: Gardina, Gardine.

GARLANDA Old French: "wreath." Var: Garlande, Garlinda.

GARNET from the gem garnet.

GAVRILA Slavic: fem. of *Gabriel*. Var. and dim: Gavra, Gavrilla.

GAY Old French: "lighthearted." Var: Gae, Gaye.

GAYORA Hebrew: "valley of light." Dim: Gaya.

GAZIT Hebrew: "of hewn stone."

GEMINA from the astrological sign Gemini. Var: Gemine, Geminia, Geminie, Gemma.

GEMMA Italian: "gem; bud."

GENEVA Old French: "juniper tree."

GENEVIEVE Celtic: "white wave." Dim: Genna, Genevra, Jenny.

GEORGIA Latin: fem. of *George*. Var. and dim: Georgene, Georgetta, Georgette, Georgiana, Georgianna, Georgie, Georgienne, Georgina, Georgine, Georgy, Giorgia.

GEORGIANA See *Georgia*.

GERALDINE Teutonic: fem. of *Gerald*. Var. and dim: Geralda, Geraldina, Gerrie, Gerry, Giralda, Jeraldine, Jerri, Jerrie, Jerry.

GERANIUM from the flower geranium.

GERDA Old Norse: "guarded; protected." Var: Garda, Gardi, Gerdie.

GERMAINE Latin: "a German." Var: Germain, Germayne.

GERTRUDE Teutonic: "spear maiden." Var. and dim: Geltruda, Gert, Gertie, Gertruda, Gerty, Truda, Trude, Trudie, Trudy.

GEULA Hebrew: "redemption."

GIBRALTA from the colony or straits of Gibraltar.

GILA Hebrew: "joy." Var: Geela, Gilana, Gilat.

GILADA Hebrew: "my joy is eternal."

GILBERTA Teutonic: fem. of *Gilbert*. Var. and dim: Gilba, Gilberte, Gilbertina, Gilbertine, Gillie, Gilly.

GILDA Celtic: "servant of God." Dim: Gillie, Gilly.

GILI Hebrew: "my joy."

GILLIAN Greek: "youthful." Var. and dim: Giliana, Giliane, Gilleta, Gillie, Gilliette, Jill.

GIMRA Hebrew: "fulfilled."

GINA See *Regina*.

GINGER See *Virginia*.

GIOVANNA Italian: fem. of *Giovanni*. Var: Gianina, Gianna.

GISELLE Teutonic: "pledge." Var: Gisela, Gisele, Gisella.

GITANA Spanish: "gypsy."

GIVA Hebrew: "hill." Var: Givona.

GLADYS Welsh: fem. var. of the Latin *Claudius*. Var. and dim: Gladdie, Gladis, Gladyse, Gleda.

GLENDA See *Glenna*.

GLENNA Gaelic: fem. of *Glenn*. Var: Glenda, Glenne, Glennis, Glynis, Glynnis.

GLORIA Latin: "glory." Var: Glo, Glori, Glory, Glorya.

GLORIANA combination of Gloria and Anne, thus "glory and grace." Var: Gloriane, Glorianna, Glorianne.

GOLDIE Teutonic: "golden-haired." Var: Golda, Goldy, Goldye.

GRACE Latin: "grace." Var. and dim: Gracia, Gracie, Gracye, Gratia, Gratiana, Grazia.

GREER Latin: fem. of *Gregory*.

GRETA, GRETCHEN, GRETEL See *Margaret*.

GRISELDA Teutonic: "gray heroine." Var. and dim: Griselle, Grizelda, Grizelle, Selda, Zelda.

GUDRUN Teutonic: daughter of the king of the Nibelungs. Var: Kudrun.

GUINEVERE Celtic: "fair lady." Var. and dim: Gaynor, Gen, Gennie, Genny, Ginevra, Guenna, Gwenore, Jen, Jennie, Jennifer, Jenny.

GURIT Hebrew: "cub." Var: Gurice.

GUSTAVA Teutonic: fem. of *Gustave*. Dim: Gussie, Gussy, Gustie.

GWENDOLEN Celtic: "white-browed." Var. and dim: Gwen, Gwenda, Gwendolyn, Gwendolynne, Gwenn, Gwenna, Gwenne, Wendi, Wendie, Wendolen, Wendy.

GWYNNE Celtic: "white; fair." Var: Gwyn, Gwyneth, Winnie, Winny.

GYPSY undetermined origin: "wanderer." Var: Gipsy.

H

HABIBAH   Arabic: "beloved." Var: Haviva.

HADARA   Hebrew: "splendid." Var: Hadura.

HADASSAH   Hebrew: "myrtle tree." Var. and dim: Dassa, Dasi, Hadass, Hadassa.

HAGAR   Hebrew: "one who flees."

HAIFA   from the city in Israel.

HALDIS   Teutonic: "purposeful." Var. and dim: Halda, Haldi, Haldisse.

HALEY   Gaelic: "ingenious."

HALIMA   Swahili/East Africa: "gentle."

HALLIE   Teutonic: dim. fem. of *Harold*. Var: Halley, Hally.

HALONA   American Indian: "happy fortune." Var: Halonna.

HALCYONE   Greek: "kingfisher bird."

HAMUDA   Hebrew: "desirable."

HANNAH   See *Anne*.

HAPPY   English: "happy." (Also see *Felicia*.)

HARALDA   Teutonic: fem. of *Harold*. Var: Halda, Harilda, Harolda, Heralda. (Also see *Hallie*.)

HARMONY   Latin: "concord." Var: Harmoni, Harmonie.

HARPER   Old English: "harp player." (Also used as a boy's name.)

HARRIET   Teutonic: "mistress of the home." Var. and dim: Harietta, Hariette, Hatti, Hattie, Hatty.

HASIA   Hebrew: "protected by God."

HASIDA   Hebrew: "pious."

HASINA   Swahili/East Africa: "good."

HATTIE   See *Harriet*.

HAWTHORN   from the hawthorn tree. Var: Hawthorne.

HAZEL   from the hazel tree.

HEATHER   from the flower heather.

HEDDA   See *Hedwig*.

HEDWIG   Teutonic: "refuge in battle." Var. and dim: Heda, Hedda, Hedva, Hedvika, Hedy.

HEDY   See *Hedwig*.

HEDYA   Hebrew: "voice of the Lord." Var: Hedia.

HEIDI   See *Hildegard*.

HELEN   Greek: "light." Var. and dim: Elaine, Elayne, Eleanor, Eleanora, Eleanore, Elinor, Elinore, Ella, Ellen, Ellene, Ellie, Ellye, Ellyne, Elnora, Helena, Helene, Hellene, Ileana, Ilona, Illona, Lena, Lenora, Lenore, Leonora, Leonore, Leora, Lina, Lora, Nell, Nella, Nellie, Nelly, Nora, Norah.

HELGA   Teutonic: "holy."

HELSA   Hebrew: "consecrated to God."

HENRIETTA   Teutonic: fem. of *Henry*. Var. and dim: Enriqua, Enriqueta, Etta, Ettie, Etty, Hattie, Hatty, Hendrika, Hennie, Henny, Henriette, Henrika, Hettie, Hetty, Netta, Nettie, Netty, Rietta, Yetta.

HEPHZIBAH   Hebrew: "my joy is in her." Var: Hephsiba, Hepsiba, Hepsibah, Hepziba, Hepzibah.

HERA   Greek: the queen of the gods.

HERMIONE   See *Erma*.

HESPER   Greek: "evening star." Var: Hespera, Hesperia.

HESTER   See *Esther*.

HIBERNIA   the old Latin name for Ireland.

HIBISCUS   from the flower hibiscus. Var: Hibisca, Hibiska.

HILA   Hebrew: "praise." Var: Hilla.

HILARY   Latin: "cheerful." Var: Hillaire, Hillary. (Also used as a boy's name.)

HILDA   See *Hildegard*.

HILDEGARD   Teutonic: "battle maid." Var. and dim: Heidi, Hilda, Hildagard, Hildagarde, Hilde, Hildegarde, Hildie, Hildy.

HILIT   Hebrew: "radiance."

HINDA   Yiddish: "deer."

HISA   Japanese: "enduring."

HOA   Vietnamese: "peace."

HOLLY   from the holly tree. Var: Hollie, Hollye.

HONORA   Latin: "honorable." Var. and dim: Honey, Honoria, Nora, Norah, Noreen, Norina, Norine.

HOPE   Old English: "hope."

HORACIA   Latin: fem. of *Horace*. Var: Horatia.

HORTENSE   Latin: "gardener." Var: Hortensa, Hortensia, Ortensia.

HOSHI   Japanese: "star."

HUBERTA   Teutonic: fem. of *Hubert*. Dim: Berta, Bertie, Berty.

HUETTE   Teutonic: fem. of *Hugh*. Var: Huetta.

HULDA   Hebrew: an Old Testament prophetess. Var: Huldah.

HYACINTH   from the flower hyacinth. Var: Hyacinthe.

HYDRANGEA   from the flower hydrangea.

HYPATIA   Greek: Beautiful and wise 5th-century philosopher and mathematician.

I

IANTHA Greek: "purple flower." Var: Ianthe.

IDA Teutonic: "happy." Var: Idalia, Idalina, Idaline, Idelle, Idette.

IDIT Hebrew: "choicest."

IDONA Teutonic: "industrious." Var: Idonah, Idonna, Iduna.

IFE Yoruba/Nigeria: "love."

IGNACIA Latin: fem. of *Ignace*. Var: Ignatia, Ignatzia.

ILKA Celtic: "industrious." Var: Ilke.

ILONA See *Helen*.

IMOGENE Latin: "image." Var: Emogene, Imogen, Imogena.

INA a Latin feminine suffix (as in Katerina), but in recent times used alone as a name.

INDIA for the country of that name.

INEZ See *Agnes*.

INGRID Swedish: "daughter." Var. and dim: Inga, Ingeborg, Inger.

IOLA Greek: "dawn cloud."

IONA Greek: "purple gem." Var: Ione, Ionia, Ionne.

IRENE Greek: "peace." Var. and dim: Eirene, Irena, Irina, Rena, Rina.

IRIS Greek: "rainbow." Var: Irisa.

IRIT Hebrew: "daffodil."

IRMA See *Erma*.

IRVINA Anglo-Saxon: fem. of *Irving*. Var: Ervina, Ervine, Ervinne, Irvetta, Irvette, Irvinne.

ISABEL Hebrew: "consecrated to God." Var. and dim: Bella, Belle, Isa, Isabella, Isabelle, Isobel, Isobella, Isobelle, Ysabel, Zabella, Zabelle.

ISADORA Greek: fem. of *Isidore*. Var. and dim: Dora, Dory, Isidora.

ISIS Egyptian goddess, sister of Osiris.

ISOLDA Celtic: "the fair." Var: Isolde.

ISRAELA Hebrew: fem. of *Israel*.

ITI Hebrew: "with me." Var: Itti.

IVANA Slavic: fem. of *Ivan* (see *John*). Var: Iva, Ivane, Ivanna, Ivanne.

IVORY from the white substance of tusks, etc.

IVY From the ivy vine.

J

JACINTA Greek: "beautiful." Var: Jacinda, Jacintha.

JACOBA Hebrew: fem. of *Jacob*. Var: Jacobah, Jacobina, Jacobine, Jakoba.

JACQUELINE French: fem. of *Jacques*. Var. and dim: Jacki, Jackie, Jacklyn, Jacky, Jacquetta, Jacquette, Jacqui.

JADA Hebrew: "wise." Var: Jadda.

JAEL Hebrew: "she-goat."

JAFIT Hebrew: "beautiful." Var: Jaffa.

JAMILA Somalia: "beautiful."

JAN See *Jane*.

JANE Hebrew: fem. of *John*. Var. and dim: Jan, Janella, Janet, Janette, Janey, Janice, Janie, Janina, Janinna, Janna, Jayne, Jean, Jeanette, Jeanie, Jeanne, Jeannette, Jeannine, Jennie, Jenny, Joan, Joana, Joanna, Joanne, Johanna, Juana, Juanita. (Also see *Giovanna*.)

JANET See *Jane*.

JANICE See *Jane*.

JARITA a bird in Hindu legend who, through her devotion to her offspring, became human.

JASMINE from the flower jasmine. Var: Jasmin, Jasmina, Jessamine, Jessamyn, Jessamyne, Yasmin, Yasmine.

JEANETTE See *Jane*.

JEMIMAH Hebrew: "dove." Var: Jemima, Jemmima.

JEMINA Hebrew: "right-handed." Var: Jamina, Yemina.

JENNIE See *Eugenia; Genevieve; Guinevere; Jane*.

JENNIFER See *Guinevere*.

JESSICA Hebrew: fem. of *Jesse*. Dim: Jess, Jesse, Jessi, Jessie, Jessy.

JEWEL Latin: "precious stone."

JILL See *Julia*.

JOAN See *Jane*.

JOCELYN Latin: "just." Var: Joceline, Jocelyne, Jocelynne, Joscelyn, Joslyn, Joslynne.

JODY See *Judith*.

JOELLE Hebrew: fem. of *Joel*. Var: Joela, Joella.

JOLIE French: "pretty."

JONINA Hebrew: "dove." Var: Yonina.

JORDANA Hebrew: fem. of *Jordan*. Var: Jordanna.

JOSEPHINE Hebrew: fem. of *Joseph*. Var. and dim: Fifi, Jo, Josefa, Josefina, Josefine, Josepha, Josephina, Josette, Josie, Pepita.

JOY Latin: "joy."

JOYCE Latin: "joyful."

JUANITA See *Jane*.

JUDITH Hebrew: "praised." Var. and dim: Jodie, Jody, Judi, Judie, Juditha, Judy.

JUDY See *Judith*.

JULIA   Greek: "youthful." Var. and dim: Giulia, Giulietta, Jill, Juliana, Juliane, Julianna, Julianne, Julie, Julienne, Juliet, Julietta, Juliette, Julina, Julita.

JULIE   See *Julia*.

JUNE   Latin: "young." Var: Junella.

JUNO   Latin: Roman goddess, the wife of Jupiter.

JUSTINE   Latin: fem. of *Justin*. Var: Giustina, Justa, Justina.

K

KADIA Hebrew: "pitcher." Var: Kadya.

KALANIT Hebrew: "anemone." Var: Kalana.

KALIFA Somalia: "holy."

KALIKA Greek: "rosebud."

KALILA Arabic: "beloved."

KALMIA New Latin: from *Kalmia latifolia*, the mountain laurel.

KAMANIA Swahili/East Africa: "like the moon."

KAREN See *Catherine*.

KARIDA Arabic: "untouched."

KARMA Sanskrit: "destiny." Var: Carma.

KAROLE See *Carol*.

KATE, KATIE See *Catherine*.

KATHERINE See *Catherine*.

KATHLEEN See *Catherine*.

KAY See *Catherine*.

KEDMA Hebrew: "toward the east." Var: Kedmah.

KEIKO Japanese: "beloved."

KELDA   Old Norse: "a spring."

KELILA   Hebrew: "crown of laurel."

KELLY   Gaelic: "warrior." (Also used as a boy's name.)

KENDRA   Anglo-Saxon: "knowing woman." Dim: Kenny.

KERRY   Gaelic: "dark one." Var: Keri, Kerri, Kerrie.

KETURAH   Hebrew: "incense." Var: Ketura.

KETZIA   Hebrew: "fragrant." Var: Katzya.

KIM   See *Kimberly*.

KIMBERLY   Old English: "from the meadow of the royal fortress." Var. and dim: Kim, Kimberley, Kimbra.

KINNERET   Hebrew: "harp."

KIRSTEN, KIRSTIN   See *Christine*.

KOHAVAH   Hebrew: "star." Var: Kohava.

KOHINOOR   Persian: "mountain of light."

KYLA   Gaelic: fem. of *Kyle*.

L

LAEL Hebrew: "devoted to the Lord." Var: Lail, Laile, Layle.

LALA Slavic: "tulip."

LALITA Sanskrit: "straightforward." Var. and dim: Lalitta, Lalittah, Lita.

LANA See *Alana.*

LANI Hawaiian: "heavenly."

LARA Latin: "renowned."

LARINA Latin: "seagull." Var: Larine.

LARISSA Greek: "cheerful." Var. and dim: Larisse, Rissa.

LATONA Latin: Roman name for the Greek goddess Leto, mother of Apollo and Diana. Var: Latonah, Latonia, Latoniah.

LAURA Latin: fem. of *Lawrence*. Var. and dim: Laureen, Laurel, Laurella, Laurelle, Lauren, Laurena, Laurene, Lauretta, Laurette, Lolly, Lora, Loralie, Lorelie, Lorella, Lorelle, Loren, Lorena,

Lorene, Loretta, Lorette, Lori, Lorie, Lorinda, Lorita, Lorna, Lorne, Lorrie, Lorry.

LAUREL See *Laura*.

LAUREN See *Laura*.

LAVERNE Old French: "springlike." Var. and dim: Laverna, LaVerna, LaVerne, Verna.

LAVINIA Latin: "woman of Rome." Var. and dim: Lavina, Lavinna, Vina, Vinia, Vinnie, Vinny.

LAYLA Swahili/East Africa: "born at night."

LEAH Hebrew: "weary." Dim: Lee, Leigh.

LEANDRA Greek: fem. of *Leander*. Dim: Lee, Leigh.

LEANNE combination of *Lee* and *Anne*, or of *Leah* and *Anne*. Var: Leana, Leane, Leanna, Liana, Liane, Lianna, Lianne.

LEATRICE combination of Lee and Beatrice.

LEDA Greek: mythological wife of Zeus, and mother of Helen and of Castor and Pollux. Var. and dim: Lee, Lida, Lyda.

LEE Old English: "of the meadow." Var: Leigh. (Also used as a boy's name.)

LEIGH See *Lee*.

LEILA Arabic: "dark as night." Var: Leela, Leilah, Leilia, Lela, Lila, Lilah.

LEILANI Hawaiian: "heavenly child; heavenly flower."

LEMUELA Hebrew: fem. of *Lemuel*. Var: Lemuella.

LENA See *Arlene*; *Helen*; *Madeline*; *Selena*.

LENORE See *Helen*.

LEONA Latin: fem. of *Leo*. Var. and dim: Lee, Leola, Leone, Leonie, Leonna, Leontine, Leontyne.

LEONARDA Teutonic: fem. of *Leonard*.

LEONORA See *Helen*.

LEONTINE See *Leona*.

LEOPOLDA Teutonic: fem. of *Leopold*. Var: Leopoldina, Leopoldine.

LEORA Hebrew: "my light." Dim: Lee.

LESLIE Celtic: "of the gray fortress." Var: Lesley. (Also used as a boy's name.)

LETITIA Latin: "joy." Var. and dim: Leta, Leticia, Letisha, Letizia, Letty, Tish, Tisha.

LEVANA Hebrew: "the moon." Var: Livana.

LEVONA Hebrew: "spice."

LIAN Hebrew: "my joy."

LIAT Hebrew: "you are mine."

LIBBY See *Elizabeth*.

LIBRA Latin: "balance."

LILAC from the flower lilac.

LILITH Arabic: "of the night." In mythology, the first wife of Adam.

LILLIAN Latin: "lily." Var. and dim: Lil, Lili, Lilia, Lilian, Liliana, Liliane, Lilla, Lilli, Lillie, Lilly, Lily, Lilyan.

LIMOR Hebrew: "myrrh." Var: Limora.

LINDA Spanish: "pretty one." Var. and dim: Lindie, Lindy, Lynda, Lynn, Lynne.

LINDEN from the linden tree.

LINDSAY Old English: "from the linden-tree island." Var: Lindsey. (Also used as a boy's name.)

LINETTE Latin: from the linnet, a song bird. Var: Linetta, Linnette, Lynette.

LIRAZ Hebrew: "my secret."

LISA See *Elizabeth*; Melissa.

LIVIA See *Olivia*.

LOIS See *Louise*.

LOLA See *Dolores*.

LORELEI Teutonic: "lurer to the rocks." Var: Lura, Lurette, Lurlene, Lurline.

LORETTA See *Laura*.

LORNA See *Laura*.

LORRAINE from the medieval kingdom of Lorraine. Var: Laraine, Larraine, Loraine, Lorayne.

LOTTA, LOTTIE See *Charlotte*.

LOTUS from the lotus flower.

LOUELLA See *Louise*.

LOUISE Teutonic: fem. of *Louis*. Var. and dim: Aloisa, Aloisia, Eloisa, Eloise, Heloise, Lois, Lou, Louella, Louisa, Louisetta, Louisette, Lu, Luella, Luisa, Luise, Lula, Lulie, Lulu.

LUBA Slavic: "lover."

LUCIANNA Latin: fem. of *Lucian*.

LUCILLE See *Lucy*.

LUCRETIA Latin: "gain; reward." Var: Lucrèce, Lucrezia.

LUCY Latin: "light." Var and dim: Cindy, Lu, Lucetta, Lucia, Lucie, Lucilla, Lucille, Lucinda, Lulu.

LUDMILLA Slavic: "loved by the people." Var. and dim: Ludmila, Millie, Milly.

LULU See *Lucy; Louise*.

LUNA Latin: "moon." Var: Lunetta, Lunette.

LYDIA Greek: "woman of Lydia." Var. and dim: Liddie, Lidia, Lydie.

LYNN Old English: "cascade." Var: Lynna, Lynne. (Also see *Linda*.)

LYRIS Greek: "of the harp or lyre." Var: Lyra, Lyrisse.

M

MAB Gaelic: the queen of the fairies in Irish mythology.

MABEL Latin: "lovable." Var. and dim: Amabel, Amabelle, Mabelle, Mae, May, Maybelle.

MADELINE Greek: "from Magdala." Var. and dim: Lena, Lina, Lynn, Lynne, Mada, Madalena, Madalene, Maddalena, Maddie, Maddy, Madelaine, Madeleine, Madelon, Madlin, Madlyn, Magda, Magdala, Magdalen, Magdalena, Magdalene, Mala, Malina, Marleen, Marlene, Marline, Marlyne.

MADGE See *Margaret*.

MAE See *May*.

MAGDALENE See *Madeline*.

MAGGIE See *Margaret*.

MAGNA Latin: fem. of *Magnus*. Dim: Maggie, Maggy.

MAGNOLIA from the flowering magnolia tree. Dim: Maggie, Maggy.

MAHALIA Hebrew: "tenderness." Var: Mahala, Mahalah, Mahaliah.

MAHIRA Hebrew: "lively." Var: Mehira.

MAIDA Anglo-Saxon: "maiden." Var. and dim: Mayda, Maydie.

MAISIE See *Margaret*.

MAJESTA Latin: another name for Maia, Roman goddess of spring. (Also see *May*.)

MALKA Hebrew: "queen." Dim: Malkie, Mollie, Molly.

MALVINA Gaelic: fem. of *Melvin*. Var: Malva, Melba, Melva, Melvina.

MAMIE See *Mary*.

MANUELA Spanish: fem. of the Hebrew *Emanuel*.

MARCELLA Latin: fem. of *Mark*. Var. and dim: Marcelle, Marcellina, Marcelline, Marcie, Marcy. (Also see *Marcia*.)

MARCIA Latin: fem. of *Mark*. Var: Marci, Marcy, Marsha. (Also see *Marcella*.)

MARGA Sanskrit: "the path."

MARGARET Latin: "pearl." Var. and dim: Gita, Gitta, Greta, Grete, Gretchen, Gretel, Grethel, Grita, Madge, Mag, Maggie, Maggy, Maisie, Marga, Margareta, Margarete, Margarita, Marge, Margery, Margherita, Margie, Margit, Margo, Margory, Margot, Marguerita, Marguerite, Margy, Marjorie, Marjory, Meg, Megan, Meta, Peg, Pegeen, Peggie, Peggy, Rita.

MARGO See *Margaret*.

MARIA, MARIE See *Mary*.

MARIANNE combination of *Mary* and *Anne*. Var: Marian, Mariana, Mariann, Marianna, Marion, Maryann, Maryanne. (Also see *Mary*.)

MARIBELLE combination of Mary and Belle, thus "beautiful Mary." Var: Marabelle, Maribel, Maribella, Marybelle. (Also see *Mary*.)

MARIGOLD from the flower marigold. Var. and dim: Goldie, Marigolda, Marigolde.

MARILYN See *Mary*.

MARINA Latin: "of the sea." Var: Marice, Maris, Marisa, Marise, Marissa, Marisse, Marna, Marni, Marnie, Marny.

MARION See *Marianne; Mary*.

MARISSA See *Marina*.

MARJORIE See *Margaret*.

MARLENE See *Madeline*.

MARNINA Hebrew: "to rejoice." Dim: Marni, Marnie.

MARSHA See *Marcia*.

MARTHA Aramaic: "lady." Var. and dim: Marta, Martella, Martelle, Marthe, Marthena, Marti, Martie, Martita, Marty, Matti, Mattie, Matty.

MARTINA Latin: fem. of *Martin*. Var. and dim: Marta, Martie, Martine, Marty, Tina.

MARVA Latin: "wonderful." Var: Marvela, Marvella, Marvelle.

MARY Hebrew: "bitter." Var. and dim: Mame, Mamie, Mara, Maralina, Maraline, Marella, Maretta, Marette, Mari, Maria, Marian, Marice, Marie, Marietta, Mariette, Marilla, Marilyn, Marilynne, Marion, Marita, Marla, Marlo, Marya, Marysa, Maryse, Maura, Maureen, Mimi, Minnie, Minny, Miriam, Mitzi, Moira, Mollie, Molly, Polly. (Also see *Marianne; Maribelle*.)

MASIKA Swahili/East Africa: "born during rain."

MATHILDA Teutonic: "brave in battle." Var. and dim: Matilda, Mathilde, Mattie, Matty, Maud, Maude, Tilda, Tillie, Tilly.

MATSU Japanese: "pine tree."

MATTEA Hebrew: fem. of *Matthew*. Var: Mathea, Mathia, Matthea, Matthia, Mattie, Matty.

MAUDE See *Mathilda*.

MAUDISA Xhosa/East Africa: "sweet one."

MAURA Latin: fem. of *Maurice*. Var: Maurilla, Maurita, Morissa, Morrisa, Morrissa.

MAUREEN See *Mary*.

MAVIS French: "thrush."

MAXINE Latin: fem. of *Maximilian*. Var. and dim: Maxene, Maxie, Maxima, Maxime, Maxy, Maxyne.

MAY Latin: from Maia, the Roman goddess of spring. Var: Mae, Maia, Maya, Maye. (Also see *Majesta*.)

MAYA Hebrew: "water."

MAYBELLE combination of May and Belle, thus "beautiful May."

MEDINA Arabic: city where the prophet Muhammad died.

MEGAN See *Margaret*.

MEHITABEL Hebrew: "favored by God." Var. and dim: Hetty, Hitty, Mehetabel, Mehitabelle.

MEI HUA Chinese: "plum blossom."

MEIRA Hebrew: fem. of *Meyer*. Var: Mira.

MELANIE Greek: "dark." Var. and dim: Melaney, Melania, Melany, Melina, Melly.

MELANTHA Greek: "dark flower."

MELBA See *Malvina*.

MELINA Greek: "honey." Var: Meleana, Melita.

MELINDA possibly a variation of *Belinda*.

MELISSA Greek: "honeybee." Var. and dim: Lisa, Lissa, Melisa, Melisse, Melita, Melitta, Mellie, Melly, Millie, Milly.

MELODY Greek: "song." Var: Melodie.

MELVINA See *Malvina*.

MERCEDES Spanish: "merciful." Var: Mercy.

MEREDITH Celtic: "protector from the sea." Var: Meridith (Also used as a boy's name.)

MERLE Latin: "blackbird." Var: Merla, Meryl, Meryle, Myrl, Myrle. (Also used as a boy's name.)

MERRIE English: "merry." Var: Merrielle, Merrilee, Merrily, Merry.

MIA Latin: "mine."

MICHAELA Hebrew: fem. of *Michael*. Var. and dim: Michaele, Michaella, Michele, Micheline, Michella, Michelle, Michelline, Mickie, Micky, Mikaela, Mikaella.

MIGNON French: "delicate." Var: Mignonne, Mignonette.

MILDRED Anglo-Saxon: "gentle." Dim: Mid, Milli, Millie, Milly.

MILLICENT Teutonic: "industrious; strong." Var. and dim: Melicent, Melisande, Melisenda, Mellicent, Milicent, Milissent, Milli, Millie, Milly.

MILLIE, MILLY See *Camilla; Emily; Mildred; Millicent*.

MIMI See *Mary*.

MIMOSA from the flower mimosa. Dim: Mim, Mimi, Mimmy.

MINERVA Latin: the Roman goddess of wisdom. Dim: Min, Minnie, Minny.

MINNA Teutonic: "loving memory." Var. and dim: Min, Mina, Mindy, Minetta, Minette, Minnie, Minny.

MINNIE See *Mary; Minerva; Minna.*

MIRABELLE Latin: "of great beauty." Var. and dim: Bella, Belle, Mira, Mirabel, Mirabella. (Also see *Myra.*)

MIRANDA Latin: "extraordinary." Dim: Randie, Randy.

MIRIAM Hebrew: "rebellious." Var. and dim: Mim, Mimi, Mimmie, Miriame, Miryam, Mitzi.

MIRTH Anglo-Saxon: "gaiety."

MITZI See *Mary; Miriam.*

MODESTA Latin: "modest." Var: Modeste, Modesty.

MOIRA See *Mary.*

MOLLY See *Malka; Mary.*

MONA Greek: "singular." Gaelic: "noble."

MONICA Latin: "adviser." Var: Monique.

MORASHA Hebrew: "inheritance."

MORELA Polish: "apricot." Var: Morella, Morelle.

MORGANA Welsh: fem. of *Morgan.*

MORIAH Hebrew: "God is my teacher." Var: Moria, Moriel, Morielle.

MOSELLE Hebrew: fem. of *Moses.* Var: Mozelle.

MURIEL Hebrew: "myrrh; bittersweet." Var: Meriel, Murielle.

MUSETTE Latin: "muse." Var: Musa, Musetta.

MYRA Latin: "wonderful." Var: Mira, Mirella, Mirelle, Myrelle, Myrilla.

MYRNA Gaelic: "gentle." Var: Merna, Mirna, Moina, Morna, Moyna.

MYRTLE from the myrtle tree. Var. and dim: Mert, Merta, Myrt, Myrta, Myrtilla, Myrtille.

N

NAAMAH Hebrew: "pleasant." Var: Naama, Naamit.

NAAVA Hebrew: "beautiful." Var: Nava, Naavit.

NADIA Russian: "hope." Var: Nada, Nadine, Nadya.

NADINE See *Nadia*.

NAIAD Latin: "water nymph."

NANCY See *Anne*.

NANETTE See *Anne*.

NAOMI Hebrew: "pleasant."

NARDA Persian: "anointed."

NASIA Hebrew: "God's miracle." Var: Nasya.

NATALIE Latin: "nativity." Var. and dim: Nat, Natala, Natalia, Nataline, Natasha, Nate, Nathalia, Nathalie, Nattie, Natty, Netta, Nettie, Netty. (Also see *Noel*.)

NATASHA See *Natalie*.

NATHANIA Hebrew: fem. of *Nathan*. Var: Natania, Tania, Tanya.

NAYO Yoruba/Nigeria: "our joy."

NEALA Gaelic: fem. of *Neal*. Var: Nealla, Neila, Neilla, Niala, Nialla, Nila.

NEDA Slavic: "born on Sunday." Var: Nedda.

NEDIVA Hebrew: "generous."

NEDRA backward spelling of *Arden*.

NEHAMA Hebrew: "comforter."

NEHANDA Zezuru/Zimbabwe: "strong."

NELDA Old English: "elder tree."

NELLIE, NELLY See *Cornelia; Helen*.

NEOMA Greek: "new moon." Var: Neomah.

NERINE Greek: "of the sea." Var: Nerice, Nerinne, Nerissa, Nerisse.

NEVA Spanish: "snow." Var: Nevada.

NEVADA for the American state. (Also see *Neva*)

NICHOLE See *Nicole*.

NICOLE Greek: fem. of *Nicholas*. Var. and dim: Nichola, Nichole, Nicholine, Nickie, Nicky, Nicola, Nicoletta, Nicolette, Nike, Niki, Nikki, Nikola.

NIKE Greek: "victory." (Also see *Nicole*.)

NILA from the river Nile.

NINA See *Anne*.

NIRA Hebrew: "light."

NIREL Hebrew: "God's light." Var: Nirelle.

NIZANA Hebrew: "bud." Var: Nitza, Nitzana.

NOBANTU Xhosa/South Africa: "popular."

NOEL French: "Christmas." Var: Noella, Noelle. (Also see *Natalie*.)

NOGA Hebrew: "morning light."

NOLA Gaelic: fem. of *Nolan*.

NOMBESE Benin/Nigeria: "wonderful child."

NOMUSA Ndebele/Zimbabwe: "merciful."

NONA Latin: "ninth (child)." Var. and dim: Nonie, Nonna, Nonnie.

NORA   See *Helen; Honora.*

NORBERTA   Teutonic: fem. of *Norbert.*

NORINE   See *Honora.*

NORMA   Old French: fem. of *Norman.*

NOVA   Latin: "new." Var: Novia.

NURIA   Hebrew: "the Lord's fire." Var: Nurya.

NURIT   Hebrew: "buttercup."

NYDIA   Latin: "refuge; nest." Var: Nidia.

OBIOMA   Igbo/Nigeria: "kind."

OCTAVIA   Latin: fem. of *Octavius*. Var. and dim: Ottavia, Tavi, Tavia.

ODELE   Greek: "melody." Var: Odelet, Odelette, Odelle.

ODELIA   Teutonic: "prosperous." Var: Odella, Odellia, Odetta, Odette.

ODERA   Hebrew: "plow."

ODESSA   from the Russian city Odessa.

OLA   Norse: fem. of *Olaf*.

OLAYINKA   Yoruba/Nigeria: "honor surrounds me."

OLGA   Teutonic: "holy."

OLIVIA   Latin: fem. of *Oliver*. Var. and dim: Livia, Olive, Olivetta, Olivette, Ollie, Olly.

OLYMPIA   Greek: "of Mt. Olympus." Var. and dim: Lympia, Olympe, Pia.

OMENA   Finnish: "apple."

OMOROSE   Benin/Nigeria: "beautiful child."

ONYX   from the banded stone onyx.

OPAL   Sanskrit: "precious stone."

OPHELIA   Greek: "help." Var. and dim: Ofelia, Ofilia, Ophelie, Phelia.

OPHIRA   Hebrew: "gold."

OPRAH   Hebrew: "young deer." Var: Ofra, Ophra.

ORA   Hebrew: "light." Var: Orah.

ORLI   Hebrew: "my light." Var: Orlit.

ORNA   Gaelic: "olive-colored." Hebrew: "cedar."

ORPAH   Hebrew: "fawn." Var: Orpa, Orpha.

OTTILIE   Teutonic: "battle heroine." Var. and dim: Otila, Otti, Ottie, Ottilia, Ottillia, Tillie, Tilly, Uta.

OVIDA   Latin: fem. of *Ovid*.

OWENA   Welsh: fem. of *Owen*.

P

PACIFICA   Latin: "peaceful."

PAGE   French: "attendant." Var: Paige.

PAKA   Swahili: "kitten."

PALLAS   Greek: "wisdom." Var: Palladia.

PALMA   Latin: "palm." Var: Palmira, Palmyra.

PALOMA   Spanish: "dove."

PAMELA   a name coined by Sir Philip Sidney in *Arcadia*, 1590. Dim: Pam.

PANDORA   Greek: "gifted." Dim: Dora.

PANSY   from the flower pansy.

PANTHEA   Greek: "from all the gods." Dim: Thea.

PARNELLA   Old French: fem. of Parnell, a form of *Peter*. Var. and dim: Nella, Parnela.

PARTHENIA   Greek: "maidenly." Var: Parthena.

PASCA   Middle English: fem. of Hebrew *Pascal*. Var: Pascalle, Pascha, Paschalle.

PAT   See *Patricia*.

PATIENCE Latin: "patience."

PATRICIA Latin: fem. of *Patrick*. Var. and dim:
Pat, Patrice, Patrizia, Patryce, Patti, Pattie, Patty,
Tricia, Trish, Trisha.

PAULA Latin: fem. of *Paul*. Var. and dim: Paulette, Paulie, Paulina, Pauline, Paulita, Pauly, Poll,
Pollie, Polly.

PAULETTE See *Paula*.

PAULINE See *Paula*.

PAZIA Hebrew: "golden." Var: Paza, Pazice, Pazit.

PEACE Latin: "peace." (Also see *Pacifica*.)

PEARL Latin: "pearl." Var. and dim: Pearla, Pearl-
ine, Perle, Perlie, Perline, Perry.

PEGGY See *Margaret*.

PELAGIA Greek: "of the sea."

PENELOPE Greek: "weaver." Dim: Pennie, Penny.

PENINA Hebrew: "coral" or "pearl." Var. and dim:
Peninah, Peninit, Penny.

PENNY See *Penelope*.

PENTHEA Greek: "the fifth (child)."

PEONY from the flower peony. Var: Peonie.

PEPITA See *Josephine*.

PERSEPHONE Greek: the daughter of Zeus, and
a personification of spring.

PERSIS Latin: "Persian woman."

PETRA Latin: fem. of *Peter*. Var. and dim: Perine,
Perrine, Pet, Petta, Petrina, Petrine, Petronella,
Petronia, Pierella, Pierelle, Pierette, Pierra.

PETULA Latin: "peevish." Var: Petulia.

PETUNIA from the flower petunia.

PHAEDRA Greek: the legendary wife of Theseus.
Var: Phedra, Phaidra.

PHILANA Greek: "lover of mankind." Var: Philene, Philida, Philina, Phillina.

PHILANTHA Greek: "lover of flowers."

PHILLIPA Greek: fem. of *Phillip*. Var. and dim: Felipa, Filippa, Phillipe, Phillipina, Phillipine, Philly, Pippa.

PHILOMENA Greek: "nightingale; lover of the moon." Var: Philomela.

PHOEBE Greek: "shining one." A title for Artemis as goddess of the moon. Var: Phebe.

PHOENICIA from the ancient country on the Mediterranean.

PHOENIX Greek: "paragon." The mythical bird that could rise from its own ashes.

PHYLLIS Greek: "green bough." Var: Philis, Phillis, Phillisse, Phylis, Phylisse, Phylyse.

PIA Italian: "devout."

PILAR Spanish: "pillar; fountain base." A Spanish name for the Virgin Mary.

PILI Swahili/East Africa: "second child."

PIPER Old English: "pipe player."

PIXIE Old English: "sprite."

PLACIDA Latin: "peaceful." Var: Placidia.

POINCIANA from the poinciana plant.

POINSETTIA from the flower poinsettia.

POLLY See *Mary*.

POMONA Latin: the Roman goddess of fruit trees.

POPPY from the flower poppy.

PORTIA Latin: "offering."

PRIMA Latin: "the first (child)."

PRIMAVERA Latin: "spring" (the season).

PRIMROSE from the flower primrose. Var: Primula.

PRISCILLA Latin: "of ancient lineage." Var. and dim: Prissie, Prisilla, Prissy.

PROSPERA Latin: "prosperous."

PRUDENCE Latin: "prudence." Dim: Pru, Prue.

PRUNELLA Latin: "plum-colored."

PSYCHE Greek: "soul."

Q

QUEENIE Teutonic: "queen." Var: Queena. (Also see *Regina*.)

QUENBY Scandinavian: "womanly." Var: Quenbie.

QUERIDA Spanish: "beloved."

QUINTINA Latin: fem. of *Quentin*. Var: Quenta, Quentina, Quinta, Quintilla.

R

RABIA Arabic: "breeze."

RACHEL Hebrew: "ewe." Var. and dim: Rachele, Rachelle, Rae, Raquel, Raquela, Raquelle, Ray, Shelly.

RADINKA Slavic: "lively."

RAE, RAY See *Rachel*.

RAINA Teutonic: "mighty." Var. and dim: Rainah, Rayna, Raynah.

RAISA See *Rose*.

RAMLA Swahili: "clairvoyant."

RAMONA Spanish: fem. of *Raymond*. Var. and dim: Mona, Raimonda, Ramonda, Ray, Romona.

RANA Sanskrit: "royal." Var: Ranee, Rani, Rania, Ranie.

RANANA Hebrew: "fresh."

RANDI Old English: fem. of *Randolph*. Var: Randelle, Randie, Randy.

RANITA Hebrew: "joy." Var: Ranit.

RAPHAELA Hebrew: fem. of *Raphael*. Var: Rafaela.

RAYANNA combination of Rachel and Anne, thus "graceful ewe." Var: Raianna, Rayanne.

RAYNA Yiddish: "pure." Var: Reyna.

RAZIA Aramaic: "secret." Var: Razi, Raziella.

REBA See *Rebecca*.

REBECCA Hebrew: "bound." Var. and dim: Becca, Becka, Becki, Beckie, Becky, Bekki, Reba, Rebeca, Rebeka, Rebekah, Rebekka, Riba, Riva, Rivkah.

REGINA Latin: "queen." Var. and dim: Gina, Regan, Reggi, Reggie, Regine, Reina, Reine, Rena, Renia, Reyna, Rina.

RENATA Latin: "reborn." Var. and dim: Renate, Rene, Renée, Reni, Renie, Rennie.

RENÉE See *Renata*.

RENITA Latin: "self-confident."

RESEDA Latin: the flower mignonette. Var: Reseta, Resetta.

RHAMA Somalia: "sweet."

RHEA Greek: "flowing." Var: Rea.

RHODA Greek: "roses" or "from the island of Rhodes." Var. and dim: Rhodie, Rhody, Roda, Rodi, Rodie, Rodina. (Also see *Rose*.)

RHONDA place name in southern Wales.

RICARDA Teutonic: fem. of *Richard*. Var. and dim: Ricca, Riccarda, Ricki, Rickie, Ricky, Riki, Rikki, Rycca.

RIESA anagram of Aries, the astrological sign.

RIMA the heroine of W. H. Hudson's *Green Mansions*.

RIMONA Hebrew: "pomegranate." Dim: Rima.

RISA Latin: "laughter." Var: Rissa.

RITA See *Margaret*.

RIVA French: "shore." Var: Reeva, Rivalee, Rivella, Rivelle.

ROANNA See *Rosanne*.

ROBERTA Old English: fem. of *Robert*. Var. and dim: Bobbi, Bobbie, Bobby, Bobbye, Bobetta, Bobette, Bobina, Robbi, Robbie, Robby, Robena, Robenia, Robin, Robina, Robine, Robinetta, Robinette, Robinia, Ruperta.

ROBIN See *Roberta*.

ROCHELLE French: "little rock." Var. and dim: Rochella, Rochetta, Rochette, Rocky, Roshella, Roshelle, Shelley, Shellie, Shelly.

RODERICA Teutonic: fem. of *Roderick*. Var. and dim: Rica, Rickie, Ricky, Rodericka.

ROHANA Hindu: "sandalwood." Var: Rohanna.

ROLANDA Teutonic: fem. of *Roland*.

ROMA Latin: the city of Rome. Var: Romana.

ROMILDA Teutonic: "famous battle maid."

RONALDA Old Norse: fem. of *Roland*. Dim: Rhona, Rona, Ronnie, Ronny.

ROSA See *Rose*.

ROSABELLE combination of Rose and Belle, thus "beautiful rose." Var: Rosabel, Rosabella.

ROSALIE See *Rose*.

ROSALIND combination of *Rose* and *Linda*. Var. and dim: Ros, Rosalinda, Rosaline, Rosalyn, Rosalynd, Rosalynn, Roselin, Roseline, Roslyn, Roz, Rozalin, Rozalind, Rozalyn, Rozlynd.

ROSAMOND Teutonic: "protectress." Var. and dim: Ros, Rosamund, Rosamunda, Rosemonde, Roz, Rozamond.

ROSANNE Combination of *Rose* and *Anne*. Var: Roanna, Roanne, Rosanna, Roseann, Roseanne.

ROSE Latin: "rose." Var. and dim: Raisa, Raizel, Rasia, Rhoda, Rhodia, Rois, Rosa, Rosalee, Rosaleen, Rosalia, Rosalie, Rosella, Roselle, Rosetta, Rosette, Rosey, Rosie, Rosina, Rosine, Rosita, Rosy, Rozalie, Rozele, Rozella, Rozelle, Zita.

ROSELLEN combination of *Rose* and *Helen*.

ROSEMARY combination of *Rose* and *Mary*. Var: Rosemarie.

ROSETTA See *Rose*.

ROWENA Old English: "famous friend." Dim: Winnie.

ROXANNE Persian: "dawn." Var. and dim: Roxana, Roxanna, Roxi, Roxie, Roxina, Roxine, Roxy.

RUBY from the gem ruby. Var: Rubetta, Rubi, Rubia, Rubie, Rubina.

RUELLA combination of *Ruth* and *Helen*. Var: Ruelle.

RUFINA Latin: fem. of *Rufus*.

RURI Japanese: "emerald." Var: Ruriko.

RUTH Hebrew: "compassionate." Dim: Ruthie.

SABA ancient country in southern Arabia. Var: Sheba.

SABINA Latin: "Sabine woman." Var. and dim: Bina, Sabine, Savina.

SABRA Hebrew: "thorny cactus; native Israeli."

SABRINA Latin: "from the boundary line." Var: Zabrina.

SACHA Russian through Greek: "helper." Var: Sasha.

SACHI Japanese: "bliss." Var: Sachiko.

SADIE See *Sarah*.

SADRIA Persian: "lotus tree."

SAKURA Japanese: "cherry blossom."

SALLY See *Sarah*.

SALOME Hebrew: "peace." Var: Salama, Saloma, Salomi, Salomie, Selima, Soloma.

SALVIA Latin: "sage" (the herb).

SAMANTHA Aramaic: "listener." Dim: Sam, Sammie, Sammy.

SAMARA Hebrew: "watchful; woman of Samaria." Dim: Mara, Sammie, Sammy.

SAMUELA Hebrew: fem. of *Samuel*. Var: Samella, Samuella, Samuelle.

SANDRA See *Alexandra*.

SANURA Swahili/East Africa: "kittenlike."

SAPPHIRA Greek: from the gem sapphire. Var: Saphira, Sapphire, Sephira.

SAPPHO the Greek lyric poetess.

SARAH Hebrew: "princess." Var. and dim: Sadie, Sadye, Sal, Sallie, Sally, Sara, Sarena, Sarene, Saretta, Sarette, Sari, Sarina, Sarine, Sarita, Shara, Shari, Zara, Zarah, Xaria.

SCARLETT from Scarlett O'Hara, the heroine of Margaret Mitchell's *Gone with the Wind*.

SEBASTIANE Latin: fem. of *Sebastian*. Var: Sebastiana, Sebastienne.

SECUNDA Latin: "the second (child)."

SELENA Greek: "the moon." Var: Celene, Celie, Celina, Celinda, Celine, Lena, Lina, Selene, Selia, Selie, Selina, Selinda, Seline.

SELIMA Arabic: "peace."

SELMA See *Anselma*.

SEPTIMA Latin: "the seventh (child)."

SERAPHINA Hebrew: "ardent; angel." Var: Serafina, Serafine, Seraphine.

SERENA Latin: "calm; serene." Dim: Rena.

SETSU Japanese: "faithful." Var: Setsuko.

SHAINA Yiddish: "beautiful." Var: Shaine, Shane, Shanie, Shayna, Shayne.

SHAMFA Somalia: "sunshine."

SHANI Swahili/East Africa: "wonderful."

SHANNON the principal river of Ireland.

SHARMA   combination of *Sharon* and *Mary*.

SHARON   Hebrew: "a plain." Var. and dim: Sharai, Sharonne, Sharrie, Sharry, Sherrie, Sherry, Sherye, and all var. and dim. of *Sarah*.

SHEBA   See *Saba*.

SHEERA   Hebrew: "song." Var: Shira, Shirah.

SHEILA   Gaelic: var. of *Cecilia*, Var: Selia, Sheela, Sheelagh, Sheilah, Shelagh, Shelley, Shelli, Shellie, Shelly. (Also see *Cecilia*.)

SHELLEY   See *Rachel*; *Rochelle*; *Sheila*.

SHERRY   See *Charlotte*; *Sharon*.

SHIFRA   Hebrew: "beautiful."

SHIRA   Hebrew: "song." Var: Shiri.

SHIRLEY   Old English: "bright meadow." Var. and dim: Sherley, Sheryl, Shirl, Shirla, Shirlee, Shirleen, Shirlene, Shirlie, Shirline, Shyrle.

SHIZU   Japanese: "quiet." Var: Shizuka, Shizuko, Shizuyo.

SHOSHANNAH   Hebrew: "rose." Var: Shoshana, Shoshanna.

SHULAMITH   Hebrew: "peaceful."

SIBYL   See *Sybil*.

SIDNEY   See *Sydney*.

SIDONIA   from the Phoenician city Sidon. Var: Sidona, Sidonie.

SIDRA   Latin: "of the stars."

SIGFREDA   Teutonic: fem. of *Siegfried*.

SIGRID   Old Norse: "beautiful victory."

SILVIA   See *Sylvia*.

SIMA   Aramaic: "treasure."

SIMBA   Swahili: "lion."

SIMCHA   Hebrew: "joy." (Also used as a boy's name.)

SIMONE Hebrew: fem. of *Simon*. Var: Simona, Simonetta, Simonette.

SIPO Ndebele/Zimbabwe: "gift."

SIVANA Hebrew: for the ninth month in the Hebrew calendar.

SIVIA Hebrew: "doe." Var: Civia, Sivie, Tzivya.

SLOAN Gaelic: "warrior." Var: Sloane. (Also used as a boy's name.)

SOLANGE Latin: "good shepherdess."

SONIA, SONYA See *Sophia*.

SOPHIA Greek: "wisdom." Var: Sofia, Sofie, Sonia, Sonja, Sonya, Sophi, Sophie, Sophronia, Sophy.

SOPHIE See *Sophia*.

SPRING English: "springtime."

STACEY See *Anastasia*; *Eustacia*.

STAR English: "star." Var: Starr.

STELLA See *Estelle*.

STEPHANIE Greek: fem. of *Stephen*. Var. and dim: Stefania, Stefanie, Steffa, Steffie, Stepha, Stephana, Stephania, Stephie, Stevana, Stevanie, Stevena, Stevenie.

STORMY English: "stormy." Var: Storm, Stormi, Stormie.

SUE See *Susan*.

SUKI Japanese: "beloved."

SUMMER English: "summer."

SUNNY English: "sunny."

SUSAN Hebrew: "lily." Var. and dim: Siusan, Sosana, Sosanna, Sosannah, Sue, Sukey, Suki, Sukie, Susana, Susanah, Susanna, Susannah, Susanne, Susetta, Susette, Susie, Susy, Suzanna, Suzanne, Suzetta, Suzette, Suzie, Suzy, Zsa Zsa.

SUSANNA, SUSANNAH See *Susan*.

SUZU Japanese: "little bell."

SVETLANA Slavic: "star." Var: Swetlana.

SWANHILDA Teutonic: "swan maiden." Dim: Hilda.

SYBIL Greek: "prophetess." Var. and dim: Sib, Sibbie, Sibby, Sibel, Sibell, Sibella, Sibelle, Sibilla, Sibille, Sibley, Sibyl, Sibyll, Sibylla, Sibylle, Sybilla, Sybille, Sybyl, Sybyla, Sybyle.

SYDNEY Old French: fem. of *Sydney*. Var. and dim: Cyd, Sid, Sidell, Sidelle, Sidna, Sidney, Sydel, Sydella, Sydelle, Sydna.

SYLVIA Latin: "of the forest." Var. and dim: Silva, Silvana, Silvia, Silvie, Syl, Sylva, Sylvana, Sylvie, Sylvya, Zilvia.

T

TABITHA Aramaic: "gazelle." Dim: Tabbi, Tabbie, Tabby.

TAKARA Japanese: "treasure."

TALIA Hebrew: "dew." Var: Talya.

TALITHA Aramaic: "maiden." Var: Taletha.

TALLULAH Choctaw Indian: "leaping water." Var. and dim: Lula, Tallie, Tallou, Tallula, Tally.

TALMA Hebrew: "hill."

TAMARA Hebrew: "palm tree." Var. and dim: Tamar, Tamma, Tammi, Tammie, Tammy.

TAMMIE, TAMMY See *Tamara; Thomasina.*

TANIA, TANYA See *Nathania; Tatiana.*

TANSY Greek: "tenacious." Var: Tansi, Tansie.

TARA Gaelic: "rocky pinnacle." Var: Tarah.

TATIANA Russian: of unknown origin. Var. and dim: Tana, Tania, Tanya, Tatyana.

TATU Swahili/East Africa: "third child."

TAURA from the astrological sign Taurus.

TAWNY Middle English: "honey-colored." Var: Tawney, Tawni, Tawnie.

TECLA Greek: "divine fame." Var: Tekla, Thecla, Thekla.

TEENA, TINA See *Christine*; *Ernestine*; *Valentina*.

TEMIMA Hebrew: "innocent."

TEMPEST Old French: "storm."

TERESA See *Theresa*.

TERRA Latin: "earth."

TERRY See *Theresa*.

TERTIA Latin: "the third (child)." Var: Terza.

TESS, TESSIE See *Theresa*.

THADDEA Greek: fem. of *Thaddeus*. Var: Thada, Thadda, Thadea.

THAIS Greek: "bond."

THALASSA Greek: "sea."

THALIA Greek: "blooming." The name of the Greek muse of comedy.

THEA Greek: "goddess."

THECLA after St. Thecla, a follower of St. Paul. Var: Tecla, Thekla.

THEDA See *Theodora*.

THELMA Greek: "nursling."

THEMA Akan/Ghana: "queen."

THEODORA Greek: fem. of *Theodore*. Var. and dim: Dora, Dori, Fedora, Feodora, Tedda, Teddi, Teddie, Teddy, Tedra, Teodora, Thea, Theda, Theo, Theodosia.

THEODOSIA See *Theodora*.

THEOLA Greek: "heaven-sent."

THEONE Greek: "godly." Var: Theona, Theonie.

THERA Greek: "untamed."

THERESA Greek: "harvester." Var. and dim: Teresa, Terese, Teresita, Teressa, Teri, Terri, Terrie, Terry, Tess, Tessa, Tessie, Tessy, Thérèse, Tracie, Tracy, Tresa, Zita.

THETIS Greek: a sea nymph, the mother of Achilles.

THIRZA Hebrew: "desirable." Var: Thyrza, Tirza, Tirzah.

THISBE Greek: "place of doves."

THOMASINA Hebrew: fem. of *Thomas*. Var. and dim: Tammi, Tammie, Tammy, Thomasa, Thomasine, Tomasina, Tomasine, Tommi, Tommie, Tommy.

THORA Teutonic: "thunder."

THYRA Greek: "shield-bearer."

TIBERIA from the river Tiber. Var: Tibera.

TIFERET Hebrew: "beautiful." Var: Tipheret.

TIFFANY Greek: "manifestation of God." Var. and dim: Tifanie, Tiffa, Tiffanie, Tiffie, Tiffy.

TIKVA Hebrew: "hope."

TILLIE, TILLY See *Mathilda*.

TIMOTHEA Greek: fem. of *Timothy*. Var. and dim: Thea, Tim, Timmi, Timmie, Timmy, Timothie.

TINA See *Valentina*.

TIRA Hebrew: "castle."

TIRZA Hebrew: "cypress."

TITANIA queen of the fairies in Shakespeare's *A Midsummer Night's Dream*.

TOBY Hebrew: fem. of *Tobias*. Var: Toba, Tobey, Tobi, Tobye, Tova, Tovah, Tovia, Tovie.

TONI, TONIA See *Antoinette*.

TOPAZ from the gem topaz.

TORI Hebrew: "my dove."

TOURMALINE from the gem tourmaline. Var: Tourmalina.

TOVA Hebrew: "she is good."

TRACY See *Theresa*.

TRICIA, TRISHA See *Patricia*.

TRINA See *Catherine*.

TRIXIE See *Beatrice*.

TRUDIE, TRUDY See *Gertrude*.

TULIA Gaelic: "peaceful." Var: Tullia.

TZIGANA Hungarian: "gypsy." Var: Tzigane, Zigana.

TZURIA Hebrew: "steadfast." Var: Tsuria, Tzuriah.

U

UDELLE Anglo-Saxon: "woman of wealth." Var: Uda, Udele, Udella.

ULA Celtic: "sea jewel." Var: Eula, Ulla.

ULANI Hawaiian: "cheerful."

ULIMA Arabic: "wise one."

ULRICA Teutonic: fem. of *Ulric*. Var. and dim: Rica, Rika, Ulrika.

UMEKO Japanese: "little plum blossom."

UNA Latin: "singular." Var: Ona, Oona.

UNDINE Latin: "wave." Var: Ondine.

UNITY Middle English: "unity."

URANIA Greek: the muse of astronomy.

URBANA Latin: "courteous."

URBI Benin/Nigeria: "princess."

URIT Hebrew: "light." Var: Urice.

URSULA Latin: "she-bear." Var. and dim: Orsa, Orsola, Ulla, Ursa, Ursala, Ursola, Ursule, Ursulina, Ursuline.

UTA See *Ottilie*.

V

VAL See *Valentina; Valerie*.

VALDA Teutonic: fem. of *Valdemar*.

VALENTINA Latin: fem. of *Valentine*. Var. and dim: Teena, Tina, Val, Vala, Vale, Valencia, Valentia, Valentine, Valli, Vallie, Vally.

VALERIE Latin: "strong; valorous." Var. and dim: Val, Valaree, Vale, Valeria, Valery, Valli, Vallie, Vally, Valora, Valoree, Valorie.

VALESKA Slavic: fem. of *Vladislav*. Var: Vladislava.

VALONIA Latin: "of the valley." Var: Vallona, Vallonia, Valona.

VANESSA Greek: "butterfly." Var. and dim: Nessa, Nessie, Nessy, Van, Vanie, Vanna, Vanni, Vannie, Vanny.

VANIA, VANYA Russian: fem. of Ivan (see *John*).

VARDA Hebrew: "rose." Var: Vardice, Vardis.

VARINA Slavic: var. of *Barbara*. Var: Varenka, Varvara, Varya, Varyusha.

VASHTI Persian: "beautiful one."

VEDA Sanskrit: "wisdom." Var: Vedis.

VEDETTA Italian: "guardian." Var: Vedette.

VEGA from the bright star Vega in the constellation Lyra.

VELDA Teutonic: "of great wisdom." Var: Valda, Valeda, Veleda.

VELMA See *Wilhelmina*.

VELVET Middle English: "velvet."

VENEZIA Italian: "Venice." Var: Venetia.

VENUS Latin: the goddess of love.

VERA Latin: "true." Russian: "faith." Var: Verena, Verene, Verina, Verine, Verita, Verity, Verla.

VERBENA from the fragrant plants of the verbena family.

VERITY Latin: "truth."

VERNA Latin: "springlike." Var: Verda, Verina, Verneta, Vernice, Vernita, Virena, Virina, Virna.

VERONICA Latin: "truthful; faithful." Var. and dim: Ranna, Ronni, Ronnie, Ronny, Veronika, Veronique, Vonni, Vonnie, Vonny.

VESPERA Latin: "evening star," or Venus.

VESTA Latin: the Roman goddess of the hearth.

VICKIE, VICKY See *Victoria*.

VICTORIA Latin: fem. of *Victor*. Var. and dim: Vicki, Vickie, Vicky, Victorina, Victorine, Viki, Vikki, Vitoria, Vittoria.

VIDONIA Portuguese: "vine branch."

VIGILIA Latin: "alert."

VINA Anglo-Saxon: "of the vine." Var: Vinna, Vinnie.

VINCENTIA Latin: fem. of *Vincent*. Var. and dim: Vincenta, Vinnie, Vinny.

VIOLET from the flower violet. Var. and dim: Vi, Viola, Violetta, Violette. (Also see *Yolanda*.)

VIRDA Latin: "fresh; blooming; green." Var: Virdis, Virida, Viridia.

VIRGILIA Latin: fem. of *Virgil*.

VIRGINIA Latin: "maidenly." Var. and dim: Ginger, Ginni, Ginnie, Ginny, Jinny, Virginie.

VITA Latin: "life." Var: Vida, Vitia.

VIVIAN Latin: "lively." Var. and dim: Vi, Viv, Vivia, Viviana, Viviane, Vivie, Vivien, Vivienne, Vivyan.

VOLETA Old French: "veiled." Var: Voletta.

W

WALDA Teutonic: fem. of *Waldo*.

WALLIS Old English: var. of boy's name *Wallace*. Dim: Wallie, Wally.

WANDA Teutonic: "wanderer." Var: Vanda, Wandie, Wandis, Wenda, Wendi, Wendie, Wendy.

WELCOME Old English: "welcome."

WENDY See *Gwendolen; Wanda*.

WENONAH American Indian: "firstborn daughter." Var. and dim: Wenona, Winnie, Winny, Winona, Winonah.

WESLA Old English: fem. of *Wesley*.

WILFREDA Teutonic: fem. of *Wilfred*. Dim: Freddie, Freddy, Willie, Willy.

WILHELMINIA Teutonic: fem. of *William*. Var. and dim: Billie, Billy, Min, Mina, Minna, Minni, Minnie, Minny, Velma, Vilma, Willa, Willamina, Willie, Willy, Wilma.

WILLOW from the willow tree.

WILLA See *Wilhelmina*.

WILMA See *Wilhelmina*.

WILONA Old English: "wished for." Var: Wilonah.

WINIFRED Teutonic: "peaceful friend." Var. and dim: Freddie, Freddy, Winnie, Winnifred, Winny.

WINOLA Old German: "gracious friend."

WYNNE Celtic: "fair; white." Var. and dim: Winnie, Winny, Wyne.

X

XANTHE Greek: "golden yellow; blond." Var: Xantha.

XAVIERA Spanish Basque: fem. of *Xavier*.

XENIA Greek: "hospitable." Var: Xena, Zena, Zenia.

XYLIA Greek: "of the forest." Var: Xyla, Xylina, Xylona.

YAFFA Hebrew: "beautiful." Var: Yafit.

YAKIRA Hebrew: "precious."

YARKONA Hebrew: "green."

YASMIN See *Jasmine*.

YEDIDA Hebrew: "beloved."

YETTA See *Henrietta*.

YEYINOU Dahomey: "glorious."

YOKO Japanese: "female."

YOLANDA Greek: "violet flower." Var: Eolande, Iolande, Iolantha, Iolanthe, Yolande, Yolantha, Yolanthe.

YOSHI Japanese: "good; respectful." Var: Yoshiko.

YVETTE See *Yvonne*.

YVONNE Old French: "archer." Var: Evonna, Evonne, Ivonna, Ivonne, Yevette, Yvette.

Z

ZABRINA See *Sabrina*.

ZAHARA Swahili: "flower."

ZAHAVA Hebrew: "golden." Var: Zahavi, Zehavit.

ZAKIYA Swahili/East Africa: "intelligent."

ZANDRA See *Alexandra*.

ZARIFA Arabic: "graceful."

ZASU after the American film star Zasu Pitts. (Meaning unknown.)

ZEBADA Hebrew: fem. of Zebadiah.

ZELDA See *Griselda*.

ZENA See *Xenia*.

ZENOBIA Greek: "given life by Zeus." Var: Zena, Zenaida, Zenda, Zenna, Zenobie.

ZERA Hebrew: "seed."

ZEVA Hebrew: fem of *Zevi*.

ZILLA Hebrew: "shadow." Var: Zillah.

ZINNIA from the flower zinnia.

ZIONA Hebrew: "excellent; woman of Zion."

ZIPPORAH   Hebrew: "sparrow." Var: Zippora.

ZITA   See *Rose; Theresa*.

ZIVA   Hebrew: "radiant." Var: Zivit.

ZOE   Greek: "life."

ZOLA   Italian: "ball of earth."

ZORA   Slavic: "dawn." Var: Zorah, Zorana, Zorina.

ZSA ZSA   See *Susan*.

ZULEIKA   Arabic: "fair one."

Boys

A

AARON Hebrew: "enlightened." Var: Aron, Haroun.

ABAYOMI Yoruba/Nigeria: "he who brings joy."

ABBOT Hebrew: "father." Var. and dim: Abbey, Abbie, Abbott, Abby, Abott.

ABDUL Arabic: "son of; servant of." Var: Abdel.

ABDULLAH Arabic: "servant of God."

ABE See *Abel; Abelard; Abraham; Abram.*

ABEL Hebrew: "breath." Dim: Abe, Abey, Abie.

ABELARD Teutonic: "resolute." Dim: Ab, Abby, Abe.

ABIJAH Hebrew: "the Lord is my father." Var: Abisha.

ABNER Hebrew: "father of light." Var. and dim: Ab, Abbie, Abby, Avner.

ABRAHAM Hebrew: "father of the multitude." Var. and dim: Abe, Abey, Abie, Abrahan, Abram, Abramo, Abran, Avram, Avrom, Bram, Brom, Ibrahim.

ABRAM Hebrew: "the lofty one is my father." The original name of Abraham. All var. and dim: of *Abraham*.

ABSALOM Hebrew: "father of peace."

ABUBAKAR Hausa/Nigeria: "noble."

ACE Latin: "unity."

ACHILLES Greek: the hero of the Trojan War. Var: Achille.

ACKERLEY Old English: "of the oak meadow." Var. and dim: Ackley, Lee, Leigh.

ADAIR Celtic: "from the oak tree ford."

ADALARD Teutonic: "brave and noble." Var: Adelard.

ADAM Hebrew: "man of the red earth." Var. and dim: Ad, Adamo, Adams, Adán, Adao, Addie, Addy.

ADAR Hebrew: "fiery."

ADDISON Old English: "son of Adam." Var. and dim: Ad, Adamson, Addie, Addis, Addy, Sonny.

ADELBERT See *Albert*.

ADELRIC Teutonic: "noble commander." Dim: Addie, Addy, Rick, Ricky.

ADIN Hebrew: "sensual."

ADJOVI Dahomey: "prince."

ADLAI Hebrew: "my witness." Dim: Ad, Addie, Addy.

ADLER Old German: "eagle."

ADOLPH Teutonic: "noble wolf." Var. and dim: Ad, Adolf, Adolfo, Adolphe, Adolpho, Adolphus, Dolf, Dolph.

ADONIS Greek: a favorite of Aphrodite. The name has come to mean "handsome."

ADRIAN Latin: "dark one." Var. and dim: Adriáno, Adrien, Hadrian, Hadriano, Iano.

ADRIEL Hebrew: "of God's congregation."

ADWIN Akan/Ghana: "artist."

AEGEUS after the Aegean Sea.

AENEAS Greek: "praiseworthy." Var: Eneas.

AEOLUS Greek: the ruler of the winds.

AFAM Akan/Ghana: "loyal."

AFFOYON Dahomey: "welcome."

AHAB Hebrew: "uncle."

AHERN Gaelic: "lord of horses." Var: Ahearn, Aherne.

AHMED Arabic: "most praised." Var: Ahmad.

AHREN Old Low German: "eagle."

AIDAN Celtic: "hearth fire." Var: Aiden.

AIKEN Anglo-Saxon: "oaken; sturdy."

AINSLEY Old English: "from the near meadow." Var. and dim: Ainslie, Lee, Leigh.

AJAX Greek: "eagle."

AKIBA, AKIVA See *Jacob.*

AKILI Tanzania: "wise one."

ALAN Celtic: "handsome; harmonious." Var. and dim: Ailin, Al, Alain, Aland, Alano, Allan, Allen, Alley, Allie, Allyn.

ALARIC Teutonic: "ruler of all." Var. and dim: Alarick, Alric, Alrick, Rick, Rickie, Ricky, Ulric, Ulrich, Ulrick.

ALASTAIR See *Alexander.*

ALBEN Latin: "white; fair." Var. and dim: Al, Alba, Alban, Albie, Albin, Albion, Alby, Alva, Alvah, Aubin, Aubyn, Benny.

ALBERN Teutonic: "noble bear." Dim: Bernie, Berny.

ALBERT Old English: "noble and brilliant." Var. and dim: Adalbert, Adelbert, Ailbert, Al, Alberto,

Albie, Albrecht, Aubert, Bert, Bertie, Berty, Delbert, Edelbert, Elbert, Ethelbert.

ALCOTT Old English: "from the old cottage."

ALDEN Old English: "old friend; protector." Var. and dim: Al, Aldin, Aldwin, Aldwyn, Elden, Eldin.

ALDO Teutonic: "rich."

ALDOUS Old English: "old; wise." Var: Aldis, Aldus.

ALDRICH Teutonic: "wise ruler." Var. and dim: Aldric, Aldridge, Alric, Audric, Eldric, Eldridge, Richie, Richy.

ALEC, ALEX See *Alexander*.

ALERON Old French: "knight."

ALEXANDER Greek: "defender of mankind." Var. and dim: Al, Alastair, Alaster, Alec, Alejandro, Aleksandr, Alessandro, Alex, Alexandre, Alexio, Alexis, Alic, Alick, Alisander, Alistair, Alister, Allister, Lex, Sander, Sandor, Sandro, Sandy, Sascha, Sasha, Saunder, Saunders.

ALEXIS See *Alexander*.

ALFONSO See *Alphonso*.

ALFORD Old English: "from the old ford."

ALFRED Old English: "elf-counselor." Var. and dim: Al, Alf, Alfie, Alfredo, Alfy, Avery, Fred, Freddie, Freddy.

ALGER Anglo-Saxon: "noble spearman." Var. and dim: Al, Algar, Algie, Algy.

ALGERNON Old French: "bearded." Var. and dim: Al, Alger, Algie, Algy.

ALI Arabic: "the highest."

ALISON Teutonic: "of sacred fame." Var: Alisen, Allison.

ALLAN See *Alan*.

110

ALLARD   Old English: "brave and noble." Var: Alard.

ALLEN   See *Alan*.

ALON   Hebrew: "oak tree."

ALONZO   See *Alphonso*.

ALOYSIUS   See *Louis*.

ALPHONSO   Teutonic: "ready for battle." Var. and dim: Al, Alf, Alfie, Alfons, Alfonso, Alfy, Alonso, Alonzo, Alphonse, Alphonsus, Fons, Fonsie, Fonz, Fonzie, Lon, Lonnie, Lonny, Lonso, Lonzo.

ALSTON   Old English: "of the noble estate."

ALTAIR   first-magnitude star in the constellation Aquila.

ALTMAN   Old German: "old man." Dim: Mannie, Manny.

ALTON   Old English: "from the old town." Var: Elton.

ALVA   See *Alben*.

ALVIN   Teutonic: "loved by all." Var. and dim: Al, Aluin, Aluino, Alvan, Alvie, Alvino, Alwin, Alwyn, Vinnie, Vinny.

ALVIS   Old Norse: "all-knowing."

AMADEO   Latin: "loved by God." Var: Amadeus, Amadis, Amadus.

AMBROSE   Greek: "immortal." Var. and dim: Ambie, Ambrogio, Ambroise, Ambros, Ambrosi, Ambrosio, Ambrosius, Brosie.

AMERIGO   after the Italian explorer Amerigo Vespucci, for whom America was named. (Also see *Emery*.)

AMORY   See *Emery*.

AMICHAI   Hebrew: "my people live."

AMIEL   Hebrew: "God of the people."

AMIN Hebrew: "faithful."

AMOS Hebrew: "burden."

AMRAM Hebrew: "a mighty nation."

ANASTASIUS Greek: "one who is reborn." Var: Anastas, Anastasios, Anastatius, Anstice, Anstiss.

ANATOLE Greek: "of the east." Var: Anatol, Anatolio.

ANDRÉ See *Andrew*.

ANDREW Greek: "manly." Var. and dim: Anders, Andie, André, Andrea, Andreas, Andrés, Andy, Drew, Dru.

ANGELO Greek: "messenger; angel." Var. and dim: Angel, Angie.

ANGUS Gaelic: "unique choice." Dim: Gus.

ANSELM Teutonic: "divine helmet." Var. and dim: Ansel, Anselme, Anselmo, Anshelm, Elmo.

ANSON Anglo-Saxon: "son of John." Var: Hanson.

ANTHONY Latin: "beyond praise." Var. and dim: Antoine, Anton, Antonin, Antonio, Antonius, Antony, Tony.

APOLLO Greek: the god of light, healing, the arts, prophecy, and manly beauty.

ARAM the Hebrew name of ancient Syria.

ARCHANGELO Greek: "principal angel." Var: Archangel.

ARCHER Old English: "bowman." Dim: Arch, Archie, Archy.

ARCHIBALD Teutonic: "truly bold." Var. and dim: Arch, Archaimbaud, Archambault, Archibold, Archiboldo, Archie, Archimbald, Archy.

ARDEN Latin: "fervent." Var. and dim: Ardie, Ardin.

ARI Hebrew: "lion."

ARIC Teutonic: "ruler." Var: Arick.

ARIEL Hebrew: "lion of God."

ARLEN Gaelic: "pledge." Var: Arlin.

ARLEY, ARLIE See *Harley*.

ARLO See *Harlow*.

ARMAND See *Herman*.

ARMSTRONG Old English: "strong of arm."

ARNIE Teutonic: "eagle." Var: Arney, Arnie.

ARNOLD Teutonic: "mighty as an eagle." Var. and dim: Arnaldo, Arnaud, Arney, Arnie, Arnoldo, Arny.

ARNON Hebrew: "rushing stream." Dim: Arnie.

ARTEMAS Greek: "gift of the goddess Artemis." Dim: Artie, Arty.

ARTHUR Celtic: "noble." Welsh: "bear-hero." Var. and dim: Art, Artair, Artie, Artur, Arturo, Artus, Arty.

ARUNDEL Old English: "of the eagle dell."

ARVAD Hebrew: "wanderer." Var. and dim: Arvid, Arvie.

ARVIN Teutonic: "friend of the people." Dim: Arv, Arvie, Arvy.

ASA Hebrew: "physician."

ASHBY Old English: "of the ash tree farm."

ASHER Hebrew: "fortunate."

ASHFORD Old English: "of the ash tree ford."

ASHLEY Old English: "from the ash tree meadow." Var. and dim: Ashleigh, Lee, Leigh. (Also used as a girl's name.)

ASHTON Old English: "from the ash tree farm." Dim: Tony.

ATHERTON Old English: "from the spring-farm." Dim: Tony.

ATLEY   Old English: "dweller in the meadow." Dim: Lee, Leigh.

ATWATER   Old English: "from the water's edge."

ATWELL   Old English: "dweller at the spring."

ATWOOD   Old English: "forest dweller." Dim: Woodie, Woody.

AUBERT   See *Albert*.

AUBIN   See *Alben*.

AUBREY   Teutonic: "elf-king." Var: Alberik, Auberon, Avery, Oberon.

AUDRIC   Teutonic: "wise ruler."

AUDWIN   Teutonic: "prosperous friend."

AUGUSTINE   See *Augustus*.

AUGUSTUS   Latin: "exalted." Var. and dim: Agosto, Aguistin, Agustin, Augie, August, Auguste, Augustin, Augustine, Austen, Austin, Gus.

AUSTEN, AUSTIN   See *Augustus*.

AVERELL   Old English: "born in April." Var: Averil, Averill.

AVERY   See *Aubrey*.

AVICHAI   Hebrew: "my father lives." Dim: Avi.

AVIDAN   Hebrew: "father of justice." Dim: Avi.

AVIEL   Hebrew: "God is my father."

AVISHALOM   Hebrew: "father of peace." Dim: Avi.

AVRAM   See *Abram, Abraham*.

AXEL   Teutonic: "father of peace." (From the Hebrew *Absalom*.) Var: Aksel.

AYLMAR, AYLMER   See *Elmer*.

AYLSWORTH   Teutonic: "of great worth."

AYLWARD   Teutonic: "noble guardian."

B

BADRU   Swahili/East Africa: "born during the full moon."

BAILEY   Old French: "steward; bailiff." Var: Baillie, Baily, Bayley.

BAINBRIDGE   Gaelic: "bridge over bright water."

BAIRD   Gaelic: "ballad singer." Var: Bard.

BALDWIN   Teutonic: "bold friend." Var: Baldovino, Balduin, Baudoin.

BALFOUR   Gaelic: "from the pastures."

BALLARD   Teutonic: "bold; strong."

BALTHASAR   one of the three wise men who brought gifts to the Christ child. Var: Baldassare, Baltasar, Balthazar.

BANCROFT   Old English: "of the bean field."

BARAK   Hebrew: "lightning."

BARAM   Hebrew: "son of the nation."

BARCLAY   Old English: "from the birch meadow." Var: Berkeley, Berkley.

BARLOW Old English: "dweller on the boar's hill."

BARNABAS Hebrew: "son of prophecy." Var. and dim: Barnaba, Barnaby, Barney, Barny.

BARNABY See *Barnabas*.

BARNARD See *Bernard*.

BARNET, BARNETT See *Bernard*.

BARNEY, BARNY See *Barnabus; Baruch; Bernard*.

BARON Teutonic: "noble warrior." Var: Barron.

BARRET Teutonic: "mighty as a bear." Var: Barrett.

BARRY Gaelic: "spear." Var: Barrie.

BART See *Barton; Bartholomew*.

BARTHOLOMEW Hebrew: "son of the furrows; farmer." Var. and dim: Bart, Bartel, Barth, Barthel, Barthelemy, Bartholome, Bartholomaus, Bartholomeus, Bartlet, Bartlett, Bartley, Bartolome, Bartolomeo, Bat.

BARTLETT See *Bartholomew*.

BARTON Old English: "from the barley farm." Dim: Bart, Tony.

BARUCH Hebrew: "blessed." Dim: Barney, Barnie, Barrie, Barry.

BARZILLAI Hebrew: "made of iron."

BASIL Latin: "kingly." Var: Basile, Basilio, Basilius, Vassily.

BAXTER Old English: "baker." Dim: Bax.

BAYARD Teutonic: "red-haired."

BEAMAN Old English: "beekeeper." Var: Beman.

BEAU French: "handsome." Var: Bo.

BEAUFORT Old French: "from the fine fortress." Dim: Beau, Bo.

BEAUMONT Old French: "of the beautiful mountain." Dim: Beau, Bo, Monty.

BEAUREGARD Old French: "of beautiful expression." Dim: Beau, Bo.

BELLAMY Old French: "fair friend."

BEN Hebrew: "son." (Also see *Benjamin* and other names beginning with Ben.)

BEN-AMI Hebrew: "son of my people."

BENEDICT Latin: "blessed." Var. and dim: Ben, Benedetto, Benedic, Benedick, Benedicto, Benedikt, Benedix, Bengt, Benito, Bennet, Bennett, Bennie, Benny, Benoit.

BENJAMIN Hebrew: "son of the right hand." Var. and dim: Ben, Beniamino, Benji, Benjie, Benjy, Bennie, Benny.

BENNETT See *Benedict*.

BENSON Hebrew-English: "son of Benjamin."

BENTLEY Old English: "of the meadow." Dim: Ben, Bennie, Benny, Lee, Leigh.

BENTON Old English: "of the moors." Dim: Ben, Bennie, Benny, Tony.

BEN-ZION Hebrew: "son of Zion." Dim: Benzi.

BERGER French: "shepherd."

BERKELEY See *Barclay*.

BERNARD Teutonic: "brave as a bear." Var. and dim: Barnard, Barnet, Barney, Barny, Bearnhard, Bern, Bernardo, Bernat, Berne, Bernhard, Bernie, Berny.

BERT Old English: "bright." Var. and dim: Bert, Bertie, Berty, Burt, Burtie, Burty. (Also see *Albert; Bertram; Berthold; Burton; Egbert; Herbert; Hubert*.)

BERTHOLD Teutonic: "brilliant ruler." Var. and dim: Bert, Bertie, Berthold, Berty.

BERTRAM Teutonic: "bright raven." Var. and dim: Bart, Bartram, Bert, Bertie, Bertrand, Bertrando, Berty.

BERWYN Old English: "bright friend." Var: Berwin.

BEVAN Celtic: "son of Evan" or "warrior's son." Var: Bevin.

BEVERLY Anglo-Saxon: "from the beaver meadow." (Also used as a girl's name.)

BEVIS Teutonic: "archer." Var: Bevus.

BILL See *William*.

BIRCH From the tree birch. Var: Burch.

BJORN Scandinavian form of *Bernard*.

BLAGDEN Old English: "from the dark valley." Var: Blagdon.

BLAINE Gaelic: "lean one." Var: Blane, Blayne.

BLAIR Gaelic: "from the plain."

BLAKE Old English: "black" or "fair," depending upon which of two root words is used. Dim: Blackey, Blacky.

BOAZ Hebrew: "strength in the Lord." Var: Boas.

BOB See *Robert*.

BOGART Teutonic: "strong as a bow." Dim: Bo, Bogey, Bogie.

BOLTON Old English: "of the manor farm." Dim: Tony.

BOND Old English: "tiller of the soil." Var: Bondon.

BONIFACE Latin: "who does good works." Var: Bonifacio, Bonifacius.

BOONE Old French: "good."

BOOTH Middle English: "of the hut." Var. and dim: Boot, Boote, Boothe, Boots.

BORDEN Old English: "of the boar valley." Dim: Bordie, Bordy.

BORG Old Norse: "from the castle."

BORIS Slavic: "fighter."

BOWEN Celtic: "son of Owen." Var: Bohen.

BOWIE   Gaelic: "yellow-haired."

BOYCE   Old French: "woodland dweller."

BOYD   Celtic: "light-haired."

BOYDEN   Anglo-Saxon: "herald." Var: Boden, Bowden.

BOYNTON   Gaelic: "from the white cow river." Dim: Tony.

BRAD   Old English: "broad." (Also used as a diminutive for names beginning with Brad.)

BRADBURN   Old English: "broad brook." Dim: Brad.

BRADEN   Old English: "of the wide valley." Dim: Brad, Brade.

BRADFORD   Old English: "from the broad ford." Dim: Brad.

BRADLEY   Old English: "from the broad meadow." Var. and dim: Brad, Bradlee, Bradleigh, Lee, Leigh.

BRADSHAW   Old English: "from the broad grove." Dim: Brad.

BRADWELL   Old English: "from the broad spring." Dim: Brad.

BRADY   Gaelic: "spirited." Var. and dim: Brad, Bradey.

BRAINARD   Old English: "bold raven." Var: Braynard.

BRAM   See See *Abraham; Bran.*

BRAMWELL   Old English: "from the well of Abraham." Dim: Bram, Brom.

BRAN   Celtic: "raven." Var: Bram.

BRAND   Old English: "fiery." Var. and dim: Bran, Brandy, Brant.

BRANDON   Old English: "from the beacon hill." Var. and dim: Bran, Branden, Brandy.

BRENDAN   Gaelic: "little raven." Var. and dim: Bren, Brendon, Brennan.

BRENT   See *Brenton.*

BRENTON   Old English: "from the steep hill." Dim: Brent, Tony.

BRETT   Celtic: "native of Brittany." Var: Bret.

BREWSTER   Old English: "brewer." Var. and dim: Brew, Brewer, Bruce, Brucie.

BRIAN   Gaelic: "strength; honor." Var: Briano, Briant, Brien, Brion, Bryan, Bryant, Bryon.

BRICE   Celtic: "quick-moving." Var: Bryce.

BRIGHAM   Old English: "dweller at the bridge."

BROCK   Old English: "badger." Dim: Broc, Brockie, Brocky, Brox.

BROCKLEY   Old English: "from the badger meadow." Dim: Brock, Lee, Leigh.

BRODERICK   Welsh: "son of Roderick." Dim: Brod, Broddie, Broddy, Rick, Rickie, Ricky. (Also see *Roderick.*)

BRODIE   Gaelic: "ditch." Var: Brody.

BROMLEY   Old English: "from the broom meadow." Var. and dim: Brom, Bromleigh, Lee, Leigh.

BRONSON   Old English: "son of the dark-skinned one." Dim: Bron, Bronnie, Bronny, Sonnie, Sonny.

BROOK   Old English: "from the brook." Var: Brooke, Brookes, Brooks.

BROUGHER   Old English: "from the fortress." Var: Brower.

BRUCE   Old French: "from the brushwood thicket."

BRUNO   Teutonic: "of dark complexion."

BRYAN, BRYANT   See *Brian.*

BUCK   Old English: "buck deer." Dim: Buckie, Bucky.

BUCKLEY   Old English: "from the buck meadow."
Dim: Buck, Buckie, Bucky, Lee, Leigh.

BUDD   Old English: "herald; messenger." Var. and
dim: Bud, Budde, Buddie, Buddy.

BUCHARD   Old English: "strong as a castle." Var.
and dim: Burch, Burckhardt, Burgard, Burkhart.

BURDETT   Old French: "little shield."

BURFORD   Old English: "from the castle ford."

BURGESS   Old English: "townsman." Dim: Burr,
Burris.

BURKE   Old French: "from the stronghold." Var.
and dim: Berk, Berke, Bourke, Burk.

BURL   Old English: "cup-bearer."

BURLEIGH   Old English: "from the castle meadow."
Var. and dim: Burley, Burlie, Lee, Leigh.

BURNE   Old English: "Brook." Var. and dim: Bernie, Berny, Bourne, Byrne.

BURR   Old Norse: "youth."

BURT   See *Bert; Burton.*

BURTON   Old English: "from the fortress." Dim:
Burt, Burtie, Tony.

BYFORD   Old English: "from the river crossing."

BYRAM   Old English: "of the cattle yard."

BYRD   Old English: "birdlike."

BYRON   Old French: "from the cottage."

C

CADELL Celtic: "of martial spirit." Var: Cadal, Cadel, Codel.

CADMAN Celtic: "warrior." Var: Cadmann, Cadmon.

CADMUS Greek: "man of the east."

CAESAR Latin: "long-haired." Var: César, Cesare.

CALDER Old English: "brook." Dim: Cal.

CALDWELL Old English: "cold stream." Dim: Cal.

CALEB Hebrew: "heart." Dim: Cal.

CALHOUN Gaelic: "from the narrow woods." Dim: Cal.

CALVERT Old English: "herdsman." Dim: Cal.

CALVIN Latin: "bald." Dim: Cal, Vinnie, Vinny.

CAMDEN Gaelic: "from the winding valley." Dim: Cam, Denny.

CAMERON Gaelic: "crooked nose." Dim: Cam, Cammie, Cammy, Ron, Ronnie, Ronny.

CAMPBELL Scotch Gaelic: "wry mouth." Dim: Cam, Campy.

CANUTE Old Norse: "knot." Var: Cnut, Knut, Knute.

CARDEW Celtic: "from the black fort."

CAREW Celtic: "from the fortress."

CAREY Welsh: "from the castle." Var: Cary.

CARL See *Charles*.

CARLETON Old English: "farmer's town." Var. and dim: Carl, Carlton, Charlie, Charlton, Charly, Tony.

CARLIN Gaelic: "little champion." Var. and dim: Carl, Carlie, Carling, Carlon, Carly.

CARLISLE Old English: "of the walled city." Var. and dim: Carl, Carlie, Carly, Carlyle, Lisle, Lyle.

CARLO, CARLOS See *Charles*.

CARMICHAEL Celtic: "of Michael's stronghold." Dim: Mickie, Micky, Mike.

CARNEY Celtic: "warrior." Var: Carny, Kearney.

CARRICK Gaelic: "of the rocky headlands."

CARROLL Celtic: "champion." Var: Carrol, Caryl.

CARSON Welsh: "marsh dweller's son." Dim: Sonnie, Sonny.

CARSWELL Old English: "dweller at the watercress spring."

CARTER Old English: "cart driver; cart-maker."

CARVELL Old English: "from the estate in the marshes." Var: Carvel.

CARVER Old English: "woodcarver."

CARY See *Carey*.

CASEY Gaelic: "valorous." (Also used as a girl's name.)

CASIMIR Slavic: "herald of peace." Var. and dim: Cass, Kasimir.

CASPER Persian: "treasurer." Var. and dim: Cash, Caspar, Cass, Cassie, Cassy, Gaspar, Gaspard, Jasper, Kaspar, Kasper.

CASS See *Casimir*; *Casper*; *Cassidy*; *Castor*.

CASSIDY Gaelic: "ingenious." Dim: Cass, Cassie, Cassy.

CASSIUS Latin: "vain." Dim: Cass, Cassie, Cassy.

CASTOR Greek: "beaver." Dim: Cass.

CATHMOR Gaelic: "great warrior." Var: Cathmore.

CATO Latin: "wise." Var: Caton, Catto, Catton.

CAVELL Teutonic: "bold." Var: Cavill.

CECIL Latin: "blind."

CEDRIC Old English: "battle chieftain." Dim: Rick, Rickie, Ricky.

CEPHAS Aramaic: "rock."

CHAD Old English: "warlike." (Also see *Chadburn*; *Chadwick*.)

CHADBURN Old English: "from the wildcat brook." Dim: Chad.

CHADWICK Old English: "from the warrior's town." Dim: Chad.

CHAIM Hebrew: "life." Var. and dim: Hy, Hyman, Hymie.

CHALMERS Scotch: "son of the overseer."

CHANDLER Old French: "candle maker." Dim: Chan.

CHANNING Old English: "knowing." Dim: Chan.

CHAPIN Old French: "chaplain." Var: Chaplin.

CHAPMAN Old English: "merchant." Dim: Chap, Chaps, Mannie, Manny.

CHARLES Teutonic: "manly." Var. and dim: Carey, Carl, Carlo, Carlos, Carrol, Carroll, Cary, Caryl, Chad, Charley, Charlie, Chas, Chaz, Chick, Chuck, Karel, Karl, Karol, Karyl.

CHARLTON see *Carleton*.

CHASE Old French: "hunter."

CHATHAM Old English: "soldier's land."

CHATWIN Old English: "soldier's friend." Dim: Winnie, Winny.

CHAUNCEY Middle English: "chancellor; church official." Var. and dim: Chance, Chancelor, Chancellor, Chancey, Chaunce.

CHEN Chinese: "great."

CHENEY Old French: "from the oak forest." Var: Chaney, Chenay.

CHESTER Old English: "from the army fort." Var. and dim: Ches, Cheston, Chet.

CHIDUKU Zezuru/Zimbabwe: "little one."

CHILTON Old English: "from the spring farm." Dim: Chil, Chilt, Tony.

CHRISTIAN Greek: "follower of Christ." Var. and dim: Chrétien, Chris, Chrissie, Chrissy, Christiano, Christie, Christy, Kit, Kris, Kristen, Kristian, Kristin.

CHRISTOPHER Greek: "Christ-bearer." Var. and dim: Chris, Chrissie, Chrissy, Christoffer, Christoph, Christophe, Christophorus, Cris, Cristobal, Cristoforo, Kit, Kris, Kriss, Kristo, Kristofor.

CHUCK See *Charles*.

CICERO Latin: "chickpea." Var: Ciceron.

CLARENCE Latin: "famous; bright." Dim: Clair, Clare.

CLARK Latin: "scholarly." Var: Clarke.

CLAUD Latin: "lame." Var: Claude, Claudian, Claudio, Claudius.

CLAUS See *Nicholas*.

CLAY Old English: "of clay."

CLAYBORNE Old English: "born of clay; mortal." Var. and dim: Claiborn, Clay, Clayborn, Claybourne, Kliborn, Kliburn.

CLAYTON Old English: "town at the clay beds." Dim: Clay, Tony.

CLEMENT Latin: "merciful; kind." Var. and dim: Clem, Clemens, Clement, Clementius, Clemmie, Clemmy, Klemens, Klement.

CLEON Greek: "famous." Var: Kleon.

CLETUS Greek: "summoned." Var. and dim: Clete, Cletis.

CLEVELAND Old English: "cliff land." Dim: Cleve, Clevie.

CLIFF Old English: "cliff."

CLIFFORD Old English: "river crossing at the cliff." Dim: Cliff.

CLIFTON Old English: "town by the cliff." Dim: Cliff, Tony.

CLINTON Old English: "from the hill farm." Dim: Clint, Tony.

CLIVE Old English: "from the cliff." Var: Cleve, Clyve.

CLYDE Celtic: "heard from afar."

COLBERT Old English: "brilliant seafarer." Var. and dim: Bert, Bertie, Berty, Cole, Colvert, Culbert.

COLBY Old English: "from the dark farm." Dim: Cole.

COLE See *Coleman*; *Colin*; *Nicholas*.

COLEMAN Celtic: "dovekeeper." Var. and dim: Cole, Colman, Manny.

COLIN Gaelic: "child." Var: Cailean, Colan, Collin. (Also see *Nicholas*.)

COLLIER Old English: "miner." Var. and dim: Colier, Colis, Collie, Collis, Colly, Collyer, Colyer.

COLTON Old English: "from the dark town." Var. and dim: Cole, Coleton, Colt, Tony.

COLUMBUS after the Italian explorer.

CONAN Celtic: "intelligent." Var. and dim: Conant, Connie, Conny.

CONLAN Gaelic: "hero." Var. and dim: Conlin, Conlon, Conney, Connie, Conny.

CONDON Celtic: "dark, wise one." Dim: Connie, Donnie.

CONRAD Teutonic: "wise counselor." Var. and dim: Con, Connie, Conny, Conrado, Curt, Konrad, Kort, Kurt.

CONROY Gaelic: "wise one." Dim: Conn, Conney, Connie, Conny, Roy.

CONSTANTINE Latin: "firm; constant." Var. and dim: Conn, Conney, Connie, Conny, Constant, Constantin, Constantino, Konstantin.

CONWAY Gaelic: "hound of the plain." Dim: Conn, Conney, Connie, Conny.

COOPER Old English: "barrel maker." Dim: Coop.

CORBETT Latin: "raven." Var. and dim: Corbet, Corbie, Corbin, Corby, Corwin, Cory.

CORCORAN Gaelic: "of ruddy complexion." Dim: Corky.

CORDELL Old French: "rope maker." Dim: Cord, Cory, Dell.

COREY Gaelic: "dweller in the ravine." Var: Cory.

CORMAC Gaelic: "charioteer." Var. and dim: Cormack, Cormick, Cory, Mac, Mickey.

CORNELIUS Latin: "horn-colored." Var. and dim: Conney, Connie, Conny, Cornel, Cornell, Cornie, Neal, Neel, Neely, Neil.

CORNELL See *Cornelius*.

CORT See *Conrad.*

CORWIN See *Corbett.*

CORYDON Greek: "lark." Var. Coridon.

COSMO Greek: "harmony; universe." Var: Cosimo, Cosmé.

COURTLAND Old English: "of the court's land." Dim: Court.

COURTNEY Old French: "of the court." Var. and dim: Cort, Court, Courtnay.

COWAN Gaelic: "of the hillside hollow." Dim: Coe.

CRAIG Gaelic: "from the crag."

CRANDALL Old English: "from the valley of cranes." Var: Crandell.

CRANLEY Old English: "from the crane's meadow." Var. and dim: Cranleigh, Cranly, Lee, Leigh.

CRANSTON Old English: "of the crane's town." Dim: Tony.

CRAWFORD Old English: "from the crow ford." Dim: Ford.

CREIGHTON Old English: "from the creek town." Var. and dim: Crichton, Tony.

CRISPIN Latin: "curly-haired." Var: Crispen, Krispin.

CRISPUS given name of Crispus Attucks, black hero of the American Revolution.

CROFTON Old English: "from the fenced farm." Dim: Croft, Tony.

CROMPTON Old English: "from the crooked farm." Dim: Tony.

CROMWELL Old English: "from the winding spring."

CROSBY Teutonic: "dweller near the cross, or cross-road." Var: Crosbey, Crosbie.

CULBERT See *Colbert.*

CULLEN   Gaelic: "handsome." Var: Cullan, Cullin.

CULVER   Old English: "dove." Var. and dim: Colly, Colver, Cully.

CURRAN   Gaelic: "champion; hero." Dim: Currey, Currie, Curry.

CURT   See *Conrad*; *Curtis*.

CURTIS   Old French: "courteous." Dim: Curt.

CUTHBERT   Old English: "famous; brilliant." Dim: Bert, Bertie, Berty.

CUTLER   Old English: "knifemaker." Dim: Cuttie, Cutty.

CYPRIAN   Latin: "man of Cyprus." Var: Ciprian.

CYRIL   Greek: "lordly." Var. and dim: Cirillo, Cirilo, Cy, Cyrill, Cyrille, Cyrillus.

CYRUS   Persian: "sun." Var. and dim: Ciro, Cy, Russ.

D

DACEY Gaelic: "southerner." Var. and dim: Dace, Dacy.

DAG Old Norse: "day; brightness."

DALE Old English: "valley dweller." (Also used as a girl's name.)

DALLAS for the city in Texas: (Also used as a girl's name.)

DALTON Old English: "from the valley town." Dim: Tony.

DALY Gaelic: "counselor." Var: Daley

DAMON Greek: "tamer; subduer." Var: Damian, Damiano, Damien, Damion.

DANA Scandinavian: "from Denmark." Var: Dane.

DANIEL Hebrew: "God is my judge." Var. and dim: Dan, Dannel, Dannie, Danny.

DANTE See *Durant*.

DANTON French: "of Anthony." Dim: Dan, Danny, Tony.

DAR Hebrew: "pearl."

DARBY Gaelic: "free man."

DARCY French: "from the stronghold." Var: Darcey, D'Arcy, Darsey, Darsy.

DARIUS Greek: "wealthy." Var: Darian, Dario, Darren.

DARNELL Old English: "from the place of hiding." Var: Darnall.

DARRELL Old French: "beloved." Var: Darrel, Darryl, Daryl.

DARREN Gaelic: "great little one." Var: Daren, Daron, Darrin, Daryn.

DARTON Old English: "from the deer park." Dim: Tony.

DARWIN after the British naturalist Charles Darwin. Dim: Winnie, Winny.

DAVID Hebrew: "beloved." Var. and dim: Dave, Davide, Davidde, Davie, Davy, Dov. (Also see *Davis*; *Dewey*.)

DAVIN Scandinavian: "bright Finn." Dim: Vinnie, Vinny.

DAVIS Old English: "son of David." Dim: Dave, Davie, Davy.

DEAN Old English: "from the valley." Var. and dim: Deane, Dino.

DEARBORN Old English: "beloved child."

DEDRICK Teutonic: "ruler of the people." Var: Deadrick, Dedric.

DELANO Old French: "from the nut tree orchard." Dim: Dell.

DELBERT See *Albert*.

DELMAR Old French: "of the sea." Var. and dim: Dell, Delmer, Delmore.

DELWYN Old English: "proud friend." Var. and dim: Dell, Delwin, Winnie, Winny, Wynn.

DEMETRIUS Greek: "follower of Demeter." Var: Demetre, Demetrio, Dmitri.

DEMPSEY Gaelic: "proud."

DEMPSTER Old English: "judge."

DENBY Scandinavian: "from the Danish settlement." Var. and dim: Danby, Dennie, Denny.

DENLEY Old English: "from the valley meadow." Dim: Dennie, Denny, Lee, Leigh.

DENNIS Greek: "of Dionysus" (god of wine and vegetation). Var. and dim: Denis, Dennet, Denney, Dennie, Denny, Denys, Dion, Dionisio, Dionysus.

DENNISON Old English: "son of Dennis." Var. and dim: Denison, Dennie, Denny, Sonny.

DENTON Old English: "from the valley farm." Dim: Dennie, Denny, Dent, Tony.

DEREK, DERRICK See *Theodoric*.

DERMOT Gaelic: "free man." Var: Dermott.

DERRY Gaelic: "red-haired."

DERWIN Teutonic: "friend of the animals." Dim: Winnie, Winny.

DESMOND Gaelic: "man of south Munster."

DEVIN Gaelic: "poet."

DEVLIN Gaelic: "fierce; valorous."

DEVON for the English county.

DEWEY Old Welsh: var. of *David*. Var: Dewie.

De WITT Old Flemish: "fair one." Var: Dewitt.

DEXTER Latin: "right-handed; dexterous." Dim: Dex.

DIBIA Igbo/Nigeria: "he who heals."

DICK See *Richard*.

DICKSON Old English: "son of Richard." Var. and dim: Dix, Dixon, Sonny.

DIEGO   See *James*.

DIETRICH   See *Theodoric*.

DILLON   Gaelic: "faithful." Dim: Dill, Dillie, Dilly.

DION   See *Dennis*.

DIRK   See *Theodoric*.

DIXON   See *Dickson*.

DMITRI   See *Demetrius*.

DOLAN   Gaelic: "dark-haired."

DOLPH, DOLPHE   See *Adolph; Randolph; Rudolph*.

DOMINIC   Latin: "the Lord's." Var. and dim: Dom, Domenic, Domenico, Domingo, Dominick, Dominik, Dominique, Nick, Nickie, Nicky, Nikki.

DONAHUE   Gaelic: "dark warrior." Dim: Don, Donn, Donnie, Donny.

DONALD   Gaelic: "world ruler." Var. and dim: Don, Donal, Donaldo, Donalt, Donn, Donnie, Donny.

DONATO   Latin: "gift." Var. and dim: Don, Donat, Donnie, Donny.

DONNELLY   Gaelic: "dark and brave." Dim: Don, Donn, Donnie, Donny.

DONOVAN   Gaelic: "dark warrior." Dim: Don, Donn, Donnie, Donny.

DORAN   Hebrew: "gift."

DORIAN   Greek: "of the sea." Dim: Dore, Dorey, Dorie, Dory.

DOTAN   Hebrew: "law."

DOUGLAS   Gaelic: "from the dark water." Var. and dim: Doug, Douglass, Dugald.

DOV   Hebrew: "bear." Dim: Dubi.

DOYLE   Gaelic: "dark stranger."

DREW   Teutonic: "trustworthy." Var: Dru. (Also see *Andrew*.)

DRISCOLL   Celtic: "interpreter."

DRUCE   Celtic: "wise man." Dim: Dru.

DRYDEN   Old English: "of the dry valley."

DUANE   Gaelic: "little dark one." Var: Dwayne.

DUDLEY   Old English: "of the people's meadow."
Dim: Lee, Leigh.

DUFF   Gaelic: "dark-haired." Dim: Duffy.

DUKE   Latin: "leader; duke."

DUNCAN   Gaelic: "dark warrior."

DUNHAM   Gaelic: "dark man."

DUNSTAN   Old English: "from the brown stone fort."
Dim: Stan.

DUNTON   Old English: "from the hill estate." Dim:
Tony.

DURANT   Latin: "enduring." Var: Dante, Durand,
Durante.

DURWARD   Old English: "gatekeeper."

DURWIN   Old English: "dear friend." Dim: Winnie,
Winny.

DUSTIN   Teutonic: "brave fighter." Dim: Dustie,
Dusty.

DWIGHT   Teutonic: "fair one." (Also see *DeWitt.*)

DYLAN   Old Welsh: "of the sea." Dim: Dill, Dillie,
Dilly.

E

EAMON See *Edmund*.

EARL Old English: "nobleman." Var. and dim: Earle, Earlie, Early, Erl, Erle, Errol, Erroll.

EATON Old English: "from the river town." Dim: Tony.

EBEN Hebrew: "stone." Dim: Eb, Ebby.

EBENEZER Hebrew: "stone of help." Dim: Eb, Eben, Ebby.

EBERHARD, EBERHART See *Everett*.

EDAN Celtic: "fiery." Dim: Ed, Eddie, Eddy.

EDEN Hebrew: "delight." (Also used as a girl's name.)

EDGAR Old English: "fortunate spearman." Var. and dim: Ed, Eddie, Eddy, Edgard, Edgardo, Ned.

EDISON Old English: "Edward's son." Var. and dim: Ed, Eddie, Eddy, Edson.

EDMUND Old English: "rich protector." Var. and dim: Eamon, Ed, Eddie, Edmon, Edmond, Edmondo, Edmundo, Ned.

EDRIC Old English: "prosperous ruler." Var. and dim: Ed, Edrick, Rick, Ricky.

EDSEL Old English: "of the rich man's estate." Dim: Ed, Eddie, Eddy.

EDWARD Old English: "prosperous guardian." Var. and dim: Ed, Eddie, Eddy, Edouard, Eduard, Eduardo, Edvard, Ned, Ted, Teddie, Teddy.

EDWIN Old English: "rich friend." Var. and dim: Ed, Eddie, Eddy, Edlin, Eduino, Ned, Winnie, Winny.

EFRON Hebrew: "bird."

EGAN Gaelic: "ardent." Var: Egon.

EGBERT Old English: "shining sword." Dim: Bert, Bertie, Berty.

EGERTON Old English: "from the hilltop town."

EINAR Teutonic: "chief."

ELBERT See *Albert*.

ELDEN Old English: "from the elf valley." Var: Eldon.

ELDRIDGE See *Aldrich*.

ELEAZAR Hebrew: "whom God hath helped." Var. and dim: El, Eli, Eleazaro, Eliezer, Ely, Lazar, Lazarus.

ELI Hebrew: "the highest." Var: Ely.

ELIAS See *Elijah*.

ELIHU See *Elijah*.

ELIJAH Hebrew: "Jehovah is my God." Var. and dim: El, Eli Eli, Elia, Elias, Elihu, Elliot, Elliott, Ellis, Ely, Ilya.

ELISHA Hebrew: "the Lord is my salvation." Var. and dim: Eli, Elisé Elisée, Eliseo, Ely.

136

ELKAN   Hebrew: "belonging to God." Var: Elkanah.

ELLARD   Old English: "noble; brave."

ELLERY   Anglo-Saxon: "from the alder tree island."
Var: Ellary, Ellerey.

ELLIOT   See *Elijah*.

ELLIS   See *Elijah*.

ELLISON   Old English: "son of Ellis." Dim: Sonnie,
Sonny.

ELSWORTH   Old English: "nobleman's estate." Var:
Ellsworth.

ELMER   Old English: "noble and famous." Var:
Aylmer.

ELMO   See *Anselm*.

ELROY   See *Leroy*.

ELSTON   Old English: "nobleman's town." Dim:
Tony.

ELVIS   Old Norse: "all-wise."

ELWIN   Old English: "the elves' friend." Var. and
dim: El, Elvin, Elvyn, Elwyn, Winn, Winnie, Winny.

ELLWOOD   Old English: "from the old forest." Var.
and dim: Elwood, Woodie, Woody.

EMERSON   Teutonic-English: "son of Emery." Dim:
Sonnie, Sonny. (Also see *Emery*.)

EMERY   Teutonic: "industrious leader." Var: Amerigo, Amery, Amory, Emmerich, Emmery, Emory.

EMIL   Teutonic: "industrious." Var: Emile, Emilio,
Emlen, Emlyn.

EMMANUEL   Hebrew: "God with us." Var. and
dim: Emanuel, Emanuele, Immanuel, Mannie, Manny, Manuel.

EMMETT   Hebrew: "truth." Anglo-Saxon: "ant."
Var: Emmet, Emmit, Emmott.

ENGLEBERT Teutonic: "bright angel." Var. and dim: Bert, Bertie, Berty, Ingelbert, Inglebert.

ENOCH Hebrew: "dedicated; consecrated."

ENOS Hebrew: "man."

EPHRAIM Hebrew: "fruitful." Var: Efraim, Efrem.

ERASMUS Greek: "lovable." Var. and dim: Erasme, Erasmo, Rasmus.

ERASTUS Greek: "beloved." Var. and dim: Eraste, Rastus.

ERHARD Teutonic: "firm resolve." Var: Erhart.

ERIC Old Norse: "ever powerful; kingly." Var. and dim: Erich, Erick, Erik, Rick, Rickie, Ricky, Rikki.

ERNEST Old English: "earnest; serious-minded." Var. and dim: Ernesto, Ernestus, Ernie, Ernst, Erny.

ERROL See *Earl*.

ERSKINE Gaelic: "from the cliff heights."

ERVIN, ERWIN See *Irving*.

ESHKOL Hebrew: "grape cluster."

ESMOND Old English: "gracious protector."

ESTES Italian: "from the east." Var: Este.

ETHAN Hebrew: "firm; strong."

EUCLID for the Greek mathematician.

EUGENE Greek: "wellborn." Var. and dim: Eugen, Eugenio, Eugenius, Gene.

EUSTACE Greek: "Rich in corn; fruitful." Var. and dim: Eustache, Eustasius, Eustazio, Eustis, Stacey, Stacie, Stacy.

EVAN Celtic: "young warrior." Var. and dim: Ev, Ewan, Ewen, Owen.

EVELYN Celtic: "pleasant."

EVERETT Old English: "strong as a boar." Var. and dim: Eberhard, Ev, Everard, Eward, Ewart.

EYAL Hebrew: "stag."

EZER Hebrew: "help."

EZEKIEL Hebrew: "God will strengthen." Var. and dim: Ezechiel, Ezequiel, Zeke.

EZRA Hebrew: "helper." Var: Esdras, Esra.

F

FABIAN   Latin: "bean grower." Var: Faber, Fabiano, Fabien, Fabio, Fabiyan.

FADIL   Arabic: "generous."

FAIRFAX   Old English: "fair-haired."

FARAJI   Swahili/East Africa: "consolation."

FARLEY   Old English: "from the sheep meadow." Var. and dim: Fairleigh, Farleigh, Farly, Lee, Leigh.

FARNHAM   Old English: "from the fern field."

FARRELL   Gaelic: "valorous." Var: Farrel, Ferrel, Ferrell.

FAULKNER   Old English: "falconer." Var: Falconer, Falkner.

FELIX   Latin: "fortunate." Var: Félice.

FELTON   Old English: "from the estate in the fields." Dim: Tony.

FENTON   Old English: "from the marshland estate." Dim: Fennie, Fenny, Tony.

FEODOR, FYODOR   See *Theodore*.

FERDINAND Teutonic: "adventuresome; strong." Var. and dim: Ferd, Ferdie, Ferdinando, Ferdy, Fergus, Fernando, Hernando.

FERGUS Gaelic: "strong man." Dim: Gus.

FERRIS Gaelic: "the rock." Var: Farris. (Also see *Peter; Pierce.*)

FIDEL Latin: "faithful." Var: Fidle, Fidelio.

FIELDING Old English: "from the field."

FILBERT Old English: "brilliant one." Var. and dim: Bert, Bertie, Berty, Filberte, Filberto, Phil, Philbert.

FILMORE Old English: "famous one." Var. and dim: Filmer, Fillmore, Morey, Phil.

FINLAY Gaelic: "fair-haired soldier." Var. and dim: Fin, Findlay, Findley, Finley, Finn, Lee.

FIRMAN Anglo-Saxon: "traveler." Dim: Manny.

FITZGERALD Old English: "son of Gerald." Dim: Fitz, Gerald, Gerry, Jerry. (Also see *Gerald.*)

FITZHUGH Old English: "son of Hugh." Dim: Fitz, Hugh. (Also see *Hugh.*)

FITZPATRICK Old English: "son of Patrick." Dim: Fitz, Pat, Patrick, Patty. (Also see *Patrick.*)

FITZROY Old English: "son of the king." Dim: Fitz, Roy.

FLEMING Old English: "Flemish."

FLETCHER Middle English: "arrow featherer." Dim: Fletch.

FLINT Old English: "stream."

FLORIAN Latin: "blooming." Var: Florio.

FLOYD See *Lloyd.*

FLYNN Gaelic: "son of the red-haired man." Var: Flinn.

FORBES Gaelic: "prosperous."

FORD Old English: "river crossing."

FORREST Old French: "forest; forest dweller." Var: Forest, Forester, Forrester, Forster, Foster.

FORTUNE Old French: "luck." Var: Fortunato, Fortunio.

FOSTER See *Forrest*.

FOWLER Old English: "gamekeeper."

FRANCIS Latin: "Frenchman." Old French: "free." Var. and dim: Chico, Francesco, Franchot, Francisco, Franciskus, Francois, Frank, Frankie, Franky, Frannie, Franny, Frans, Franz, Paco, Pancho.

FRANK See *Francis*.

FRANKLIN Middle English: "freeholder." Var. and dim: Francklin, Francklyn, Frank, Frankie, Franklyn, Franky.

FRANZ See *Francis*.

FRAZER Old English: "curly-haired." Var: Fraser, Frasier, Frazier.

FRED See *Frederick*.

FREDERICK Teutonic: "peaceful ruler." Var. and dim: Federico, Federigo, Fred, Freddie, Freddy, Frederic, Frederich, Frederico, Frederik, Fredric, Fredrick, Friedrich, Fritz, Rick, Rickie, Ricky.

FREELAND Old English: "from the free land."

FREEMAN Old English: "free man." Dim: Manny.

FREEMONT Teutonic: "protector of freedom." Dim: Monty.

FRITZ See *Frederick*.

FULLER Middle English: "cloth worker."

FULTON Old English: "from the farm town." Dim: Tony.

G

GABRIEL   Hebrew: "God is my strength." Var. and dim: Gabbie, Gabby, Gabe, Gabriele, Gabriello, Gaby.

GAD   Hebrew: "happy." Dim: Gadi.

GAGE   Old French: "pledge."

GALE   Old English: "lively; gay." Var: Gail.

GALEN   Gaelic: "bright little one."

GALI   Hebrew: "mountain." Var: Galya.

GALLAGHER   Gaelic: "eager helper."

GALVIN   Gaelic: "sparrow." Var. and dim: Galvan, Galven, Vinnie, Vinny.

GAMALIEL   Hebrew: "God is my reward."

GANNON   Gaelic: "of fair complexion."

GARDNER   Middle English: "gardener." Var. and dim: Gard, Gardener, Gardie, Gardiner, Gardy.

GARETH   See *Garrett*.

GARFIELD   Old English: "battlefield." Dim: Gar, Garf.

GARLAND   Old English: "from the battlefield." Old French: "wreath." Var. and dim: Gar, Garlan, Garlen.

GARNER   Teutonic: "guardian warrior."

GARON   Hebrew: "threshing floor." Var: Guryon.

GARRETT   Old English: "mighty with a spear." Var: Gareth, Garrard, Garret, Garreth, Gary. (Also see *Gerald*; *Gerard*.)

GARRICK   Old English: "spear-king." Dim: Gary, Rick, Rickie, Ricky.

GARSON   Hebrew: "stranger." Var. and dim: Gerson, Gershom, Gershon, Sonny.

GARTH   Old Norse: "gardener."

GARVEY   Gaelic: "rough peace."

GARVIN   Old English: "friend in battle." Var. and dim: Garv, Garwin, Vinnie, Vinny, Win, Winnie, Winny.

GARWOOD   Old English: "from the fir forest." Dim: Woodie, Woody.

GARY   Old English: "spear carrier." Var: Garey, Garry. (Also see *Garrett*; *Garrick*.)

GASPAR   See *Casper*.

GASTON   French: "man of Gascony." Dim: Tony.

GAVIN   Welsh: "white hawk." Var: Gavan, Gaven, Gawain, Gawen.

GAYLORD   Old French: "spirited one." Var. and dim: Galer, Gallard, Galliard, Gay, Gayelord, Gayler, Gaylor.

GAYNOR   Gaelic: "son of the fair-haired man." Var. and dim: Gainer, Gainor, Gay, Gayner.

GEDALIA   Hebrew: "God is great." Var: Gedaliah.

GENE   See *Eugene*.

GEOFFREY Teutonic: "God's peace." Var. and dim: Geof, Geoff, Godfrey, Gottfried, Jeff, Jeffers, Jeffie, Jeffrey, Jeffry, Jeffy.

GEORGE Greek: "farmer." Var. and dim: Geordie, Georg, Georges, Georgie, Georgy, Giorgio, Joji, Jorge, Jurgen, Yuri.

GERALD Teutonic: "mighty spearman." Var. and dim: Garald, Garold, Gary, Gearalt, Geraud, Gerrald, Gerrie, Gerry, Giraldo, Giraud, Jerald, Jerold, Jerrie, Jerrold, Jerry. (Also see *Garrett; Gerard.*)

GERARD Old English: "brave spearman." Var. and dim: Gearard, Gerardo, Geraud, Gerhard, Gerhardt, Gerrie, Gerry, Gherardo. (Also see *Garrett*; *Gerald.*)

GERSHOM See *Garson.*

GIBOR Hebrew: "hero."

GIDEON Hebrew: "warrior; feller of trees."

GIFFORD Old English: "brave giver." Var. and dim: Giff, Giffard, Gifferd, Giffie, Giffy.

GILBERT Teutonic: "bright pledge." Var. and dim: Bert, Bertie, Berty, Burt, Gibb, Gibbie, Gibby, Gil, Gilberto, Gilburt, Gilly, Giselbert, Guilbert, Wilbert, Wilbur, Wilburt, Will, Willy.

GILBY Gaelic: "yellow-haired lad." Var. and dim: Gil, Gilbey.

GILCHRIST Gaelic: "pledged to Christ." Dim: Gil, Gill, Gillie, Gilly.

GILEAD Arabic: "camel hump." (a mountainous region east of the Jordan River) Var: Gilad, Giladi.

GILES Greek: "shield-bearer." Var: Egide, Egidio, Gide, Gilles.

GILMORE Gaelic: "servant of the Virgin Mary." Var. and dim: Gil, Gill, Gillie, Gillmore, Gilly, Gilmour, Morey.

GILROY Latin: "faithful to the king." Dim: Gil, Gill, Gillie, Gilly, Roy.

GIOVANNI See *John*.

GIUSEPPE See *Joseph*.

GIVON Hebrew: "heights."

GLADWIN Old English: "cheerful friend." Dim: Win, Winn, Winnie, Winny.

GLEN Gaelic: "valley." Var: Glenn, Glyn, Glynn.

GLENDON Gaelic: "from the valley fortress." Dim: Don, Donnie, Donny, Glen, Glenn.

GODDARD Teutonic: "divinely firm." Var: Godard, Godart, Goddart, Gotthard, Gotthart.

GODFREY See *Geoffrey*.

GODWIN Old English: "good friend." Var. and dim: Goodwin, Win, Winnie, Winny.

GOLDWIN Old English: "golden friend." Var. and dim: Goldwyn, Win, Winnie, Winny.

GORDON Old English: "from the three-cornered hill." Var. and dim: Gordan, Gorden, Gordie, Gordy.

GOWER Old Welsh: "pure."

GRADY Gaelic: "illustrious."

GRAHAM Teutonic: "from the gray house."

GRANT Latin: "great."

GRANTHAM Old English: "from the great meadow." Dim: Grant.

GRANTLAND Old English: "from the great plain." Dim: Grant.

GRANVILLE Old French: "from the great town or estate."

GRAYSON Old English: "judge's son." Dim: Sonnie, Sonny.

GREGORY Greek: "vigilant." Var. and dim: Greer, Greg, Gregg, Gregoire, Gregor, Gregorio, Gregorius.

GRESHAM Old English: "from the grazing lands."

GRIFFITH Old Welsh: "fierce chief; ruddy." Dim: Griff, Griffie, Griffy.

GRISWOLD Teutonic: "from the gray forest."

GROVER Old English: "from the grove." Dim: Grove.

GUIDO See *Guy*.

GUNTHER Old Norse: "warrior." Var: Gunnar, Gunner, Gunter.

GURIEL Hebrew: "God is my lion."

GUS See *Augustus; Gustave*.

GUSTAVE Teutonic: "staff of the Goths." Var. and dim: Gus, Gustaf, Gustav, Gustavo, Gustavus.

GUTHRIE Gaelic: "from the windy place." Teutonic: "war hero."

GUY French: "guide." Var: Guido.

H

HADAR Hebrew: "adornment."

HADDEN Old English: "from the moors." Var: Haddon.

HADLEY Old English: "from the heath meadow." Var. and dim: Haddie, Hadleigh, Lee, Leigh.

HADRIAN See *Adrian*.

HADWIN Old English: "friend in war." Dim: Win, Winnie, Winny.

HAGEN Gaelic: "young, little one." Var: Hagan.

HAINES Teutonic: "from the hedged enclosure." Var: Haynes.

HAKON Old Norse: "of the noble race."

HAL See *Harold; Henry*.

HALDEN Old Norse: "half Danish." Var: Haldan.

HALE Old English: "dweller at the hall." Var: Hall.

HALEY Gaelic: "ingenious."

HALFORD Old English: "from the river-crossing manor."

HALIL   Turkish: "close friend."

HALLAM   Old English: "from the hillside."

HALLEY   Old English: "from the manor meadow." Dim: Lee, Leigh.

HALSEY   Old English: "from Hal's island." Var. and dim: Hal, Halsy.

HALSTEAD   Old English: "from the manor." Var. and dim: Hal, Halsted, Steady.

HAMAL   Arabic: "lamb."

HAMILTON   Old English: "from the mountain estate." Dim: Tony.

HAMISH   See *James*.

HAMLIN   Old French-German: "little home-lover."

HANFORD   Old English: "from the high ford." Var. and dim: Hanleigh, Lee, Leigh.

HANIF   Arabic: "believer."

HANS   See *John*.

HARCOURT   Old French: "fortified dwelling." Dim: Harry.

HARDEN   Old English: "from the hare valley." Dim: Denny.

HARDY   Teutonic: "bold; daring."

HAREL   Hebrew: "God's mountain."

HARITH   Arabic: "plowman." Var: Harithah.

HARLAN   Old English: "from the battle land." Var: Harland, Harlin.

HARLEY   Old English: "from the hare's meadow." Var. and dim: Arley, Harleigh, Lee, Leigh.

HARLOW   Old English: "from the fortified hill." Var: Arlo.

HARMON   See *Herman*.

HAROLD   Old Norse: "army ruler." Var. and dim: Araldo, Hal, Harald, Harry, Herold.

HAROUN   Arabic form of *Aaron*.

HARPER   Old English: "harp player." (Also used as a girl's name.)

HARRIS   Old English: "son of Harry." Var: Harrison.

HARRY   See *Harold; Henry*.

HART   Old English: "stag."

HARTLEY   Old English: "of the deer meadow." Dim: Hart, Lee, Leigh.

HARTWELL   Old English: "from the deer's spring."

HARVEY   Teutonic: "warrior." Var. and dim: Harv, Hervey.

HASKEL   probably a Yiddish form of *Ezekiel*. Var: Haskell.

HASSAN   Arabic: "handsome."

HAVELOCK   Old Norse: "sea battle."

HAWLEY   Old English: "from the hedged meadow." Dim: Lee, Leigh.

HAYDEN   Old English: "from the hedged valley." Var: Haydon.

HAYES   Old English: "from the hedged place."

HAYWARD   Old English: "keeper of the hedged enclosure."

HAYWOOD   Old English: "from the hedged forest." Var. and dim: Heywood, Woodie, Woody.

HEATH   Middle English: "of the heath."

HECTOR   Greek: "steadfast." Var: Ettore.

HENRY   Teutonic: "ruler of an estate." Var. and dim: Enrico, Enrique, Hal, Hank, Harry, Heindrick, Heinrich, Heinrik, Hendrik, Hennie, Henny, Henri, Henrik.

HERBERT   Teutonic: "bright warrior." Var. and dim: Bert, Bertie, Berty, Erberto, Harbert, Hebert, Herb, Herbie, Herby, Heriberto.

HERMAN Teutonic: "warrior." Var. and dim: Armand, Armando, Armin, Ermin, Ermanno, Harman, Harmon, Hermann, Hermie, Hermon.

HERNANDO See *Ferdinand.*

HERSHEL Hebrew: "deer." Var: Hersch, Herschel, Hersh, Herzel, Heschel, Heshel, Hirsch.

HEWITT Teutonic: "little Hugh." Var. and dim: Hewie, Hewett. (Also see *Hugh.*)

HEYWOOD See *Haywood.*

HILARY Latin: "cheerful." Var. and dim: Hilaire, Hilario, Hilarius, Hill, Hillary, Hillery, Hillie, Hilly, Ilario. (Also used as a girl's name.)

HILLEL Hebrew: "greatly praised."

HILLIARD Teutonic: "brave warrior." Var: Hillier, Hillyer.

HILTON Old English: "from the hill estate." Var. and dim: Hylton, Tony.

HIRAM Hebrew: "most noble." Dim: Hi, Hy.

HIROSHI Japanese: "generous."

HOBART See *Hubert.*

HOD Hebrew: "vigor."

HOGAN Gaelic: "youth."

HOLBROOK Old English: "from the brook in the hollow." Var. and dim: Brook, Brooke, Holbrooke.

HOLCOMB Old English: "from the deep valley."

HOLDEN Teutonic: "kindly."

HOLLIS Old English: "from the holly grove."

HOLMES Middle English: "from the river islands." Var: Holman, Holmann.

HOLT Old English: "of the forest."

HOMER Greek: "pledge." Var: Homère, Homerus, Omero.

HORACE Latin: "keeper of the hours." Var: Horacio, Horatio, Horatius, Orazio.

HORATIO See *Horace.*

HORTON Old English: "from the gray estate." Dim: Tony.

HOSEA Hebrew: "salvation."

HOUGHTON Old English: "from the cliff estate." Dim: Tony.

HOUSTON Old English: "from the hill town." Dim: Hugh, Hugie, Tony.

HOWARD Old English: "guardian." Dim: Howie.

HOWELL Old Welsh: "alert." Var. and dim: Howe, Howie.

HOWLAND Old English: "from the highlands." Dim: Howie.

HUBERT Teutonic: "bright-minded." Var. and dim: Bert, Bertie, Berty, Burt, Hobard, Hobart, Huberto, Hubie, Hugh, Hughie, Uberto.

HUDSON for the Hudson River.

HUGH Old English: "intelligent." Var. and dim: Huey, Hughes, Hughie, Hugo, Ugo.

HULBERT Teutonic: "grace and brilliance." Dim: Bert, Bertie, Berty, Burt, Hulbard, Hulburt.

HUMBERT Teutonic: "bright home." Var. and dim: Bert, Bertie, Berty, Burt, Umberto.

HUME Teutonic: "home."

HUMPHREY Teutonic: "man of peace." Var: Humfrey, Humfried, Hunfredo, Onofredo.

HUNTER Old English: "hunter." Dim: Hunt.

HUNTINGTON Old English: "hunting estate." Var. and dim: Hunt, Huntingdon, Tony.

HUNTLEY Old English: "from the hunter's meadow." Dim: Hunt, Lee, Leigh.

HURD Anglo-Saxon: "hard."

HURLEY Gaelic: "sea-tide."

HUSSEIN Arabic: "small and handsome."

HUTTON Old English: "from the house on the ridge." Dim: Tony.

HUXLEY Old English: "from Hugh's meadow." Dim: Hux, Lee, Leigh.

HYATT Old English: "from the high gate." Var. and dim: Hiatt, Hy.

HYMAN Hebrew: "life." Var. and dim: Chaim, Hayyim, Hy, Hymie, Mannie, Manny.

I

IAN See *John*.

IBRAHIM Arabic form of *Abraham*.

ICHABOD Hebrew: "departed glory."

IGNATIUS Latin: "ardent; fiery." Var. and dim: Iggie, Iggy, Ignace, Ignacio, Ignaz, Ignazio, Inigo.

IGOR Scandinavian: "hero."

IMMANUEL See *Emmanuel*.

INGEMAR Old Norse: "famous son." Var: Ingmar.

INGER Old Norse: "the son's army." Var: Ingar, Ingvar.

INGRAM Teutonic: "angel raven." Var: Ingraham.

INNIS Gaelic: "from the river island." Var: Innes, Inness.

IRA Hebrew: "the watchful."

IRVIN, IRVINE See *Irving*.

IRVING Gaelic: "handsome; fair." Var. and dim: Erv, Ervin, Erwin, Irv, Irvin, Irvine, Irwin.

IRWIN See *Irving*.

ISAAC Hebrew: "he laughs." Var. and dim: Ike, Isac, Isaak, Isacco, Isak, Itzik, Izzy, Yischak.

ISAIAH Hebrew: "God is salvation." Dim: Izzy.

ISHMAEL Hebrew: "God will hear."

ISIDORE Greek: "gift of Isis." Var. and dim: Dore, Dory, Isador, Isadore, Isidor, Isidoro, Isidro, Izzy.

ISRAEL Hebrew: "wrestling with the Lord." Dim: Izzy.

ISSACHAR Hebrew: "there is a reward."

ITAI Hebrew: "friendly." Var: Ittai.

ITIEL Hebrew: "God is with me."

ITTAMAR Hebrew: "island of palm; gracefulness."

IVAN See *John*.

IVAR Old Norse: "archer." Var: Iver, Ives, Ivor, Yves, Yvon.

JABARI Swahili/East Africa: "courageous."

JACK See *Jacob*; *John*.

JACKSON Old English: "Jack's son." Dim: Jack, Sonny.

JACOB Hebrew: "supplanter." Var. and dim: Akiba, Akiva, Cob, Cobb, Cobbie, Cobby, Giacobo, Giacomo, Giacopo, Hamish, Jack, Jackie, Jacky, Jacobo, Jacques, Jaime, Jake, Jakie, Jay, Jock.

JACQUES See *Jacob*; *James*.

JAFAR Arabic: "little stream."

JAHI Swahili/East Africa: "dignified."

JAMES English: var. of *Jacob*. Var. and dim: Diego, Giacomo, Hamish, Iago, Jacques, Jaime, Jamesy, Jamey, Jamie, Jay, Jayme, Jemmie, Jemmy, Jim, Jimmie, Jimmy, Jock, Jocko, Seamus, Seumas, Shamus.

JAMIL Arabic: "handsome."

JAN See *John*.

JARED   See *Jordan.*

JAROSLAV   Czech: "glory of spring."

JARVIS   Teutonic: "spear-sharp." Var: Jarvey, Jervis.

JASCHA   Russian: dim. of *Jacob* and *James.*

JASON   Greek: "healer." Dim: Jay, Sonny.

JASPER   See *Casper.*

JAY   from the birds called jays. (Also see *Jacob*; *James*; *Jason.*)

JEAN   See John.

JED   Arabic: "hand." (Also see *Jedidiah.*)

JEDIDIAH   Hebrew: "beloved of the Lord." Dim: Jed.

JEFFERSON   Old English: "Jeffrey's son." Dim: Jeff, Jeffie, Jeffy.

JEFFREY   See *Geoffrey.*

JELANI   Swahili/East Africa: "powerful."

JENNINGS   Anglo-Saxon: "descendants of John."

JEREMIAH   Hebrew: "God will uplift." Var. and dim: Geremia, Jere, Jereme, Jeremias, Jeremy, Jerry.

JEREMY   See *Jeremiah.*

JERMYN   Latin: "a German." Dim: Jerry.

JEROLD, JERROLD   See *Gerald.*

JEROME   Latin: "sacred name." Var. and dim: Gerome, Gerry, Hieronymus, Jerrome, Jerry.

JESS   See *Jesse.*

JESSE   Hebrew: "wealthy." Dim: Jess, Jessie.

JETHRO   Hebrew: "abundance." Dim: Jeth.

JIM   See *James.*

JOAB   Hebrew: "God is the father."

JOACHIM   Hebrew: "God will judge." Var: Akim, Joaquin.

JOEL   Hebrew: "Jehovah is the Lord."

JOHANN   See *John.*

JOHN Hebrew: "God has been gracious." Var. and dim: Evan, Ewan, Gian, Giovanni, Hans, Ian, Ivan, Jack, Jackie, Jacky, Jan, Janos, Jean, Jen, Jens, Jock, Jocko, Johan, Johann, Johannes, Johnnie, Johnny, Jon, Jonnie, Juan, Sean, Shaughn, Shaun, Shawn, Zane.

JOJI Japanese form of *George*.

JONAH Hebrew: "dove." Var: Jonas.

JONAS See *Jonah*.

JONATHAN Hebrew: "God has given." Dim: Jon, Jonnie.

JORDAN Hebrew: "descending." Var. and dim: Giordano, Jared, Jordie, Jori, Jory, Jourdain.

JOSÉ See *Joseph*.

JOSEPH Hebrew: "he shall increase." Var. and dim: Che, Giuseppe, Iosep, Jo, Joe, Joey, José, Josef, Pepe.

JOSH See *Joshua*.

JOSHUA Hebrew: "Jehovah is my salvation." Dim: Josh.

JOSIAH Hebrew: "the Lord's fire." Var: Josias.

JOTHAM Hebrew: "God is perfect."

JUAN See *John*.

JUBAL Hebrew: "ram's horn."

JUDAH Hebrew: "praised." Var: Judd, Jude, Yehuda, Yehudah, Yehudi.

JUDD See *Judah*.

JUDSON Old English: "Judah's son."

JULES See *Julian; Julius*.

JULIAN Latin: "belonging to Julius." All var. and dim. of *Julius*.

JULIUS Greek: "youthful; downy-bearded." Var. and dim: Giulio, Jule, Jules, Julie, Julio.

JUNIUS Latin: "youthful."

JURGEN See *George*.

JUSTIN Latin: "upright; just." Var: Giustino, Giusto, Justinian, Justino, Justis, Justus.

K

KADAR Arabic: "powerful." Var: Kedar.

KADIN Arabic: "companion."

KADMIEL Hebrew: "God is the ancient One."

KALIL Hebrew: "crown; wreath."

KAMIL Arabic: "perfect."

KANE Celtic: "bright." Var: Kain, Kayne.

KARIM Arabic: "generous."

KARL See *Charles.*

KASIMIR See *Casimir.*

KASPER See *Casper.*

KATRIEL Hebrew: "the Lord's crown."

KEANE Middle English: "sharp." Celtic: "handsome." Var: Kean, Keen, Keene.

KEEFE Gaelic: "handsome; lovable."

KEEGAN Gaelic: "ardent little one." Var: Kegan.

KEENAN Gaelic: "little old one." Var: Kienan.

KEIR Celtic: "dark-skinned."

KEITH Welsh: "of the forest."

KELLY Gaelic: "warrior." Var: Kelley. (Also used as a girl's name.)

KELSEY Teutonic: "dweller by the water."

KENDALL Old English: "from the bright valley." Var. and dim: Ken, Kendal, Kendell, Kennie, Kenny.

KENDRICK Gaelic: "Henry's son." Dim: Ken, Kennie, Kenny, Rick, Rickie, Ricky.

KENLEY Old English: "from the royal meadow." Var. and dim: Ken, Kenleigh, Kennie, Kenny, Lee, Leigh.

KENNEDY Gaelic: "helmeted." Dim: Ken, Kennie, Kenny.

KENNETH Celtic: "handsome." Dim: Ken, Kennie, Kenny.

KENT Old Welsh: "bright; white." Dim: Ken, Kennie, Kenny.

KENWAY Old English: "bold in battle." Dim: Ken, Kennie, Kenny.

KENYON Gaelic: "fair-haired." Dim: Ken, Kennie, Kenny.

KERMIT Gaelic: "free man."

KERRY Gaelic: "dark." Var: Kerr.

KEVIN Gaelic: "handsome." Var: Kevan, Keven.

KIERAN Gaelic: "little dark one." Var: Kiernan.

KIM Old English: "chief." (Also see *Kimball*.)

KIMBALL Anglo-Saxon: "royally brave." Var. and dim: Kim, Kimbell, Kimble.

KING Old English: "ruler."

KINGSLEY Old English: "from the king's meadow." Var. and dim: King, Kingsleigh, Kinsley, Lee, Leigh.

KINGSTON Old English: "from the king's estate." Dim: King, Tony.

KIPP Old English: "from the pointed hill." Dim: Kippie, Kippy.

KIRBY   Old Norse: "from the church town." Var: Kerby.

KIRK   Old Norse: "of the church."

KIT   See *Christian; Christopher*.

KLAUS   See *Nicholas*.

KNOX   Old English: "of the hills."

KNUT, KNUTE   See *Canute*.

KOHAV   Hebrew: "star."

KRISPIN   See *Crispin*.

KUMI   Akan/Ghana: "strong."

KURT   See *Conrad*.

KYLE   Gaelic: "handsome."

L

LABAN Hebrew: "white."

LAIRD Celtic: "proprietor; landlord."

LAMAR Spanish: "the sea." Teutonic: "land famous."

LAMBERT Teutonic: "bright land." Var. and dim: Bert, Bertie, Berty, Lamberto.

LAMONT Old Norse: "lawyer." Var. and dim: Lammond, Lamond, Monty.

LANCE Latin: "helper." Var: Lancelot, Launcelot.

LANDIS Old French: "from the grassy plain." Var: Landers.

LANE Middle English: "from the lane." Dim: Lanny.

LANG Old Norse: "tall one."

LANGDON Old English: "from the long hill." Var. and dim: Donny, Landon, Lang, Langsdon, Langston.

LANGLEY Old English: "from the long meadow." Var. and dim: Langleigh, Lee, Leigh.

LARRY See *Lawrence.*

LARS See *Lawrence*.

LARSON Scandinavian: "Lars' son." Dim: Sonny.

LATHAM Teutonic: "dweller by the barns."

LATHROP Anglo-Saxon: "from the low village."

LATIMER Middle English: "interpreter." Dim: Lattie, Latty.

LAUREN, LAURENCE See *Lawrence*.

LAVI Hebrew: "lion."

LAWFORD Old English: "from the ford on the hill." Dim: Ford.

LAWRENCE Latin: "crowned with laurel." Var. and dim: Larry, Lars, Lauren, Laurence, Laurens, Laurent, Laurie, Lauritz, Lawrance, Lawrie, Lon, Lonnie, Lonny, Lorant, Loren, Lorens, Lorenzo, Lorin, Lorrie, Lorry.

LAWSON Old English: "son of Lawrence." Dim: Sonnie, Sonny.

LAWTON Old English: "from the hill town or hill estate." Dim: Tony.

LAZAR, LAZARUS See *Eleazar*.

LEANDER Greek: "lion-man." Var. and dim: Ander, Leandro, Lee.

LEE Old English: "from the meadow." Var: Leigh. (Also used as a girl's name.)

LEIF Old Norse: "beloved." Var: Lief.

LEIGH See *Lee*.

LEIGHTON Old English: "from the meadow estate." Var. and dim: Layton, Leigh, Tony.

LEITH Celtic: "wide river."

LELAND Old English: "meadowland." Dim: Lee, Leigh.

LEMUEL Hebrew: "consecrated to God." Dim: Lem, Lemmie, Lemmy.

LENNOX Scottish place name. Dim: Len, Lenny.

LEO Latin: "lion." Var. and dim: Lee, Leon, Lev, Lion, Lionel, Lyon, Lyonel. (Also see *Leonard*, *Leopold*.)

LEON See *Leo*.

LEONARD Teutonic: "bold as a lion." Var. and dim: Lee, Len, Lenard, Lennard, Lennie, Lenny, Léonard, Leonerd, Leonhard, Leonid, Leonidas, Lonnard, Lonnie, Lonny. (Also see *Leo*.)

LEOPOLD Teutonic: "defender of the people." Dim: Leo.

LEROY French: "the king." Var. and dim: Elroy, Lee, Leigh, Leroi, Roy.

LESLIE Gaelic: "from the gray fortress." Var. and dim: Lee, Leigh, Les, Lesley. (Also used as a girl's name.)

LESTER Latin: "from the camp or legion." Dim: Les.

LEV See *Leo*.

LEVI Hebrew: "joined in devotion."

LEWIN Old English: "beloved friend." Dim: Lew.

LEWIS See *Louis*.

LIAM Gaelic form of *William*.

LINCOLN Celtic: "from the settlement by the pool." Dim: Linc, Link.

LINDBERG Teutonic: "from the linden tree hill." Dim: Lindy.

LINDLEY Old English: "of the linden tree meadow." Var. and dim: Lee, Leigh, Lindleigh, Lindy.

LINDSAY Old English: "from the linden tree island." Var: Lindsey. (Also used as a girl's name.)

LINUS Greek: "flaxen-haired."

LIONEL See *Leo*.

LIRON Hebrew: "the song is mine."

LLEWELLYN Old Welsh: "lionlike." Var. and dim: Lew, Llewelyn, Llywellyn.

LLOYD Old Welsh: "gray-haired." Var: Floyd.

LOGAN Gaelic: "from the hollow."

LOMBARD Teutonic: "long-beard." Dim: Bard.

LON See *Alphonso*; *Lawrence*.

LOREN, LORENZO See *Lawrence*.

LORIMER Latin: "harness-maker." Var. and dim: Lorrie, Lorrimer, Lorry.

LORING Teutonic: "famous in war." Dim: Lorrie, Lorry.

LOTAN Hebrew: "to protect."

LOUIS Teutonic: "renowned warrior." Var. and dim: Aloysius, Lew, Lewis, Lodovico, Lou, Louie, Ludvig, Ludwig, Luigi, Luis.

LOWELL Old English: "beloved." Old French: "little wolf." Var: Lovell.

LUCAS See *Lucius*.

LUCIAN Greek: Meaning unknown, but possibly related to *Lucius*. Var: Luciano, Lucien.

LUCIUS Latin. "bringer of light." Var. and dim: Luc, Luca, Lucas, Luce, Lucias, Lucio, Luck, Lucky, Lukas, Luke. (Also see *Lucian*.)

LUDWIG See *Louis*.

LUIS See *Louis*.

LUKE See *Lucius*.

LUTHER Teutonic: "famous warrior." Var: Lothaire, Lothar, Lothario, Lutero.

LYDELL Old English: "from the wide dell." Dim: Dell.

LYLE Old French: "of the island." Var: Lisle.

LYMAN Old English: "man of the meadows."

LYNDON Old English: "from the linden tree hill."
   Var. and dim: Lindon, Lindy, Lynn.
LYNN Old English: "waterfall." Var: Lin, Linn, Lyn.
LYSANDER Greek: "liberator." Dim: Sander, Sandy.

M

MAC Celtic: "son of." A diminutive of names beginning with Mac, Max, Mc. Var: Mack.

MacADAM Gaelic: "son of Adam." Var. and dim: Adam, Mac, Mack, McAdam. (Also see *Adam*.)

MacDONALD Gaelic: "son of Donald." Var. and dim: Don, Donald, Mac, Mack, McDonald. (Also see *Donald*.)

MacKENZIE Gaelic: "son of the wise leader." Var. and dim: Ken, Mac, Mack, McKenzie.

MACY Old English: "mace-bearer." Var: Macey.

MADDOCK Celtic: "beneficent." Var: Maddox.

MADISON Old English: "warrior's son." Dim: Maddie, Maddy, Sonnie, Sonny.

MAGNUS Latin: "great." Var: Manus.

MAHLULI Ndebele/Zimbabwe: "victorious."

MAIMON Aramaic: "good fortune."

MAITLAND Old English: "of the meadows."

MALACHI Hebrew: "my messenger; the Lord's messenger." Var: Malachy.

MALCOLM Arabic: "dove." Gaelic: "follower of St. Columba." Dim: Mal.

MANDEL Teutonic: "almond." Dim: Mannie, Manny.

MANFRED Teutonic: "man of peace." Dim: Fred, Freddie, Freddy, Mannie, Manny.

MANGWIRO Zezuru/Zimbabwe: "bright."

MANNING Teutonic: "son of the good man." Dim: Mannie, Manny.

MANUEL See *Emmanuel*.

MANVILLE Old French: "from the great estate." Var. and dim: Mannie, Manny, Manvel, Manvil.

MARC See *Mark*.

MARCEL Latin: "little Mark." (Also see *Mark*.)

MARCUS See *Mark*.

MARDEN Old English: "from the valley of the pool."

MARIO See *Mark*.

MARION Hebrew: var. of girl's name *Mary*.

MARK Latin: "warlike." Var: Marc, Marco, Marcos, Marcus, Mario, Marius, Markos, Markus.

MARLAND Old English: "from the boundary."

MARLON See *Merlin*.

MARLOW Old English: "from the hill by the lake." Var: Marlo, Marlowe.

MARSDEN Old English: "from the marsh valley." Dim: Denny.

MARSHALL Teutonic: "military commander." Var. and dim: Marsh, Marshal.

MARTIN Latin: "warlike." Var. and dim: Mart, Marten, Martie, Martino, Marty, Martyn.

MARUNDA Tanzania: "industrious."

MARVIN Old English: "sea friend." Var. and dim: Marv, Merv, Mervin, Merwin, Merwyn, Murvyn, Myrvyn, Myrwyn.

MASON Old French: "stone worker." Dim: Sonnie, Sonny.

MASUD Swahili/East Africa: "lucky."

MATATA Tanzania: "noisy one."

MATT See *Matthew*.

MATTHEW Hebrew: "gift from God." Var. and dim: Mat, Mateo, Mathias, Matias, Matt, Matteo, Mattheus, Matthias, Matthieu, Mattie, Matty.

MAURICE Latin: "dark-skinned." Var. and dim: Mauricio, Maurie, Maurise, Maurits, Maurizio, Maury, Morey, Morie, Moritz, Morris.

MAX See *Maximilian; Maxwell*.

MAXIMILIAN Latin: "the greatest." Var. and dim: Mac, Mack, Massimiliano, Massimo, Max, Maxey, Maxie, Maxim, Maximilianus, Maximilien, Maximo, Maxy.

MAXWELL Old English: "from the great man's well." Dim: Mac, Mack, Max, Maxey, Maxie, Maxim, Maxy.

MAYER See *Meyer*.

MAYNARD Teutonic: "strong." Var: Menard.

MEAD Old English: "from the meadow." Var: Meade.

MEDWIN Teutonic: "powerful friend." Dim: Winnie, Winny.

MEGED Hebrew: "goodness."

MELBOURNE Old English: "from the mill stream." Var. and dim: Mel, Melburn, Milburn, Millburn.

MELVIN Celtic: "chief." Var. and dim: Mal, Malvin, Mel, Melvyn, Vinnie, Vinny.

MENACHEM Hebrew: "comforter." Var. and dim: Mannes, Mannie, Manny, Menahem.

MENASSEH Hebrew: "causing to forget."

MENDEL Latin: "of the mind." Dim: Dell.

MEREDITH Celtic: "protector from the sea." (Also used as a girl's name.)

MERLE French: "blackbird." (Also used as a girl's name.)

MERLIN Anglo-Saxon: "falcon." Var. and dim: Marlen, Marlin, Marlon, Merl, Merle.

MERRILL Teutonic: "famous." Var. and dim: Merill, Merle, Meryl.

MERTON Old English: "from the place by the sea." Dim: Tony.

MERVIN See *Marvin*.

MEYER Teutonic: "farmer." Hebrew: "bringer of light." Var: Mayer, Meier, Meir, Myer.

MICHAEL Hebrew: "who is like God." Var. and dim: Micah, Michal, Michail, Micheil, Michel, Michele, Mickey, Mickie, Miguel, Mikael, Mike, Mikel, Mikey, Mikkel, Mischa, Mitch, Mitchel, Mitchell.

MILES Latin: "warrior." Var: Milo, Myles.

MILFORD Old English: "from the mill crossing." Var: Millford.

MILLARD Old English: "miller." Var: Miller, Millman, Milman.

MILLS Old English: "of the mills."

MILO See *Miles*.

MILSON Old English: "son of Miles."

MILTON Old English: "of the mill town." Dim: Milt, Miltie, Milty.

MIRUMBI Rwanda: "born during the rain."

MISCHA See *Michael*.

MITCHELL See *Michael.*

MOHAMMED See *Muhammad.*

MONROE Celtic: "from the red marsh." Var: Monro, Munro, Munroe.

MONTAGUE French: "from the pointed mountain." Dim: Monte, Monty.

MONTE See *Montague; Montgomery.*

MONTGOMERY Old French: "from the rich man's mountain." Dim: Monte, Monty.

MOORE Old French: "dark-complected." (Also see *Maurice.*)

MORDECAI Hebrew: "warrior." Var. and dim: Mord, Mordechai, Mordie, Mordy, Mort, Mortie, Morty.

MOREY See *Maurice; Murray; Seymour.*

MORGAN Gaelic: "sea-white."

MORLEY Old English: "from the moor meadow." Dim: Lee, Leigh.

MORRIS See *Maurice.*

MORRISON Old English: "son of Maurice." Dim: Sonnie, Sonny. (Also see *Maurice.*)

MORSE Old English: "son of Maurice." (Also see *Maurice; Moore.*)

MORTIMER Old French: "dweller by the still water." Dim: Mort, Mortie, Morty.

MORTON Old English: "from the estate on the moor." Dim: Mort, Mortie, Morty, Tony.

MOSES Hebrew: "saved." Var. and dim: Moe, Moisé, Moises, Mose, Moshe, Moss.

MOSHE See *Moses.*

MOSI Swahili/Tanzania: "firstborn."

MOSS See *Moses.*

MUHAMMAD Arabic: "praised." Var. Mohammed.

172

MUIR Celtic: "of the moors."

MUNROE See *Monroe*.

MUNYARADZI Zezuru/Zimbabwe: "comforter."

MURDOCK Celtic: "prosperous seaman."

MURRAY Celtic: "sailor." Var: Morey, Murry.

MYLES See *Miles*.

MYRON Greek: "fragrant; pleasant." Dim: Ron, Ronnie, Ronny.

N

NAAMAN Hebrew: "pleasant; agreeable." Var: Naamann, Naman.

NADAV Hebrew: "benefactor."

NAHUM Hebrew: "compassion."

NAMIR Hebrew: "leopard."

NAPHTALI Hebrew: "to wrestle." Var: Naftali.

NAPOLEON Greek: "lion of the woodland dell." Dim: Leon, Nappie, Nappy.

NATHAN Hebrew: "gift." Dim: Nat, Nate.

NATHANIEL Hebrew: "gift of God." Var. and dim: Nat, Natanael, Nataniel, Nate, Nathanael.

NAVON Hebrew: "wise."

NEAL See *Neil*.

NED See *Edmund; Edward*.

NEHEMIAH Hebrew: "the Lord's compassion."

NEIL Gaelic: "champion." Var: Neal, Neale, Neall, Nealon, Neel, Neill, Neils, Nels, Nial, Niall, Niel, Niels, Niles, Nils.

NELSON Celtic: "son of Neil." Var: Nealson, Nilson. (Also see *Neil*.)

NEMO Greek: "from the glen."

NESTOR Greek: "the wise."

NEVILLE Old French: "new town." Var: Nevil, Nevile.

NEVIN Old English: "nephew." Var. and dim: Nev, Nevins, Niven, Vinnie, Vinny.

NEWBOLD Old English: "from the new building."

NEWTON Old English: "from the new estate."

NICHOLAS Greek: "victory of the people." Var. and dim: Claus, Colas, Cole, Colet, Colin, Klaus, Niccolo, Nichols, Nick, Nickie, Nickolaus, Nicky, Nicol, Nicolai, Nicolas, Niki, Nikita, Nikki, Nikolas, Nikolaus, Nikolos.

NICODEMUS Greek: "conqueror of the people." Dim: Nick, Nickie, Nicky.

NIGEL Latin: "dark; black."

NIMROD Hebrew: "rebel; hunter." Dim: Nim.

NIRIEL Hebrew: "God's field." Var: Nirel.

NISSAN Hebrew: "flight."

NISSIM Hebrew: "sign; miracle."

NIXON Old English: "son of Nicholas."

NOAH Hebrew: "rest; peace."

NOAM Hebrew: "sweetness."

NOBLE Latin: "wellborn."

NOEL French: "Christmas." Var: Natal, Natale, Nowell.

NOLAN Celtic: "noble; famous." Var: Noland.

NORBERT Teutonic: "divine brightness." Dim: Bert, Bertie, Berty.

NORMAN Teutonic: "man of the north; man of Normandy." Var. and dim: Norm, Normand, Norris.

NORRIS See *Norman*.

NORTHROP Old English: "from the north farm."

NORTON Old English: "from the northern town." Dim: Tony.

NORVILLE Old French: "from the northern estate."

NORWARD Old English: "northern guardian." Dim: Ward.

NORWELL Old English: "from the north spring."

NORWOOD Old English: "from the northern forest." Dim: Woodie, Woody.

NURI Hebrew: "fire."

NYE Middle English: "islander."

O

OAKES Old English: "of the oak trees." Dim: Oakie.

OAKLEY Old English: "from the oak tree meadow." Dim: Lee, Leigh.

OBADIAH Hebrew: "servant of God." Var. and dim: Obadias, Obed, Obediah, Obie, Oby.

OCTAVIUS Latin: "the eighth (child)." Var: Octave, Octavian, Octavio, Octavus.

ODELL Old Norse: "wealthy one." Dim: Dell, Odey, Odie, Ody.

OFER Hebrew: "young deer."

OGDEN Old English: "from the oak valley." Dim: Denny.

OHIN Akan/Ghana: "chief."

OJEMBA Igbo/Nigeria: "traveler."

OKON Ibibio/Nigeria: "born at night."

OLAF Old Norse: "ancestral relic." Var. and dim: Olav, Ole, Olen, Olin.

OLIVER Latin: "olive tree." Var. and dim: Noll, Nollie, Nolly, Olivero, Olivier, Oliviero, Ollie, Olly, Olvan.

OLUJIMI Yoruba/Nigeria: "God's gift."

OMAR Arabic: "first son; most high; follower of the Prophet." Var: Omer.

OMRI Arabic: "long life."

ORDWAY Anglo-Saxon: "spear fighter."

OREN Hebrew: "cedar or fir tree." Gaelic: "pale-skinned." Var: Oran, Orin, Orren, Orrin.

ORFORD Old English: "from the cattle ford."

ORESTES Greek: "man of the mountains." Var: Oreste.

ORION Greek: "son of fire."

ORLANDO See *Roland*.

ORMOND Old English: "from the bear mountain."

ORSON Latin: "bearlike." Var. and dim: Sonnie. Sonny, Ursen.

ORTON Teutonic: "man of wealth." Var: Orten.

ORVILLE French: "golden town."

OSBERT Old English: "divinely bright." Dim: Bert, Bertie, Berty.

OSBORN Old English: "divinely strong." Var. and dim: Osborne, Osbourne, Ozzie, Ozzy.

OSCAR Old Norse: "divine spear." Var. and dim: Oskar, Ossie, Ozzie, Ozzy.

OSGOOD Old English: "divinely good." Dim: Ozzie, Ozzy.

OSMER Teutonic: "divine fame." Var: Osmar.

OSMOND Teutonic: "divine protection." Var. and dim: Osmund, Ozzie, Ozzy.

OSWALD Old English: "divine power." Var. and dim: Ossie, Ossy, Oswell, Ozzie, Ozzy, Waldo. (Also see *Waldo*.)

OTIS Greek: "keen of hearing."
OTTO Teutonic: "wealthy."
OVID Latin: "shepherd."
OWEN See *Evan*.
OZ Hebrew: "strength." Var: Ozni.

P

PABLO See *Paul*.

PADRAIC See *Patrick*.

PAGE French: "attendant." Var: Padget, Padgett, Paget, Paige.

PAINE Latin: "a rustic." Var: Payne.

PALMER Old English: "bearing palms; a pilgrim."

PALTI Hebrew: "deliverance."

PARKER Old English: "keeper of the park." Var. and dim: Park, Parke.

PARNELL See *Peter*.

PARRY Welsh: "son of Harry."

PASCAL Hebrew: "to pass over; born at Passover or Easter." Var: Pascale, Paschal, Pasquale.

PATRICK Latin: "of noble birth." Var. and dim: Paddie, Paddy, Padraic, Pat, Paton, Patrice, Patricio, Patrizio, Patsy, Patten, Pattie, Patty, Payton, Peyton, Rick, Rickie, Ricky.

PAUL Latin: "small." Var. and dim: Pablo, Paley Paolo, Paulie, Pauly, Pavel, Poul.

PAXTON Teutonic: "pack man; itinerant trader." Var. and dim: Packston, Packton, Paxon, Tony.

PAYNE See *Paine*.

PAYTON See *Patrick*.

PEARCE See *Peter*.

PEARSON Old English: "son of Peter." Var. and dim: Pierson, Sonnie, Sonny.

PEDRO See *Peter*.

PEMBROKE Welsh: "from the headland."

PENROD Teutonic: "famous commander." Dim: Penn, Pennie, Penny, Rod, Roddie, Roddy.

PERCIVAL Old French: "valley-piercer." Var. and dim: Parsifal, Perceval, Percy.

PERCY See *Percival*.

PEREGRINE Latin: "wanderer." Dim: Perry.

PERRY Middle English: "pear tree." Var: Parry. (Also see *Peter*.)

PETER Greek: "rock." Var. and dim: Farris, Ferris, Parnell, Parry, Peadar, Pearce, Peder, Pedro, Peirce, Perkin, Perren, Perrin, Perry, Pete, Petey, Petie, Petrus, Pierce, Piero, Pierre, Pieter, Pietro.

PEYTON See *Patrick*.

PHELAN Celtic: "wolf."

PHELPS Old English: "son of Philip."

PHIL See *Filbert; Filmore; Philip*.

PHILEMON Greek: "loving."

PHILETUS Greek: "worthy of love."

PHILIP Greek: "lover of horses." Var. and dim: Felipe, Filip, Filippo, Phil, Phillip, Phillipe.

PHILO Greek: "love."

PHINEAS Hebrew: "oracle."

PIERCE See *Peter*.

PIERRE See *Peter*.

PIERREPONT French: "stone bridge." Var: Pier-pont.

PINCHAS Hebrew: "dark-skinned." Var: Pincus.

PLATO Greek: "broad-shouldered." Var: Platon.

POLLARD Teutonic: "brave one."

POLLOCK Old English: "little Paul."

POMEROY Old French: "of the apple orchard." Dim: Roy.

PORTER Latin: "gatekeeper." Dim: Terry.

POWELL Old Welsh: "son of Howell." (Also see *Howell*.)

PRENTICE Middle English: "apprentice." Var: Prentiss.

PRESCOTT Old English: "from the priest's cottage." Dim: Scott, Scottie, Scotty.

PRESLEY Old English: "from the priest's meadow." Var. and dim: Lee, Leigh, Pressley, Priestley.

PRESTON Old English: "of the priest's town." Dim: Press, Tony.

PRICE Welsh: "son of the ardent one."

PRIMO Italian: "first; firstborn."

PRIOR Latin: "superior; head of a monastery." Var: Pryor.

PROCTOR Latin: "administrator."

PROSPER Latin: "to prosper." Var: Prospero.

PUTNAM Anglo-Saxon: "dweller at the pond."

QUARTUS Latin: "the fourth (child)."

QUENTIN Latin: "the fifth (child)." Var. and dim: Quent, Quinn, Quint, Quintin, Quinton, Quintus.

QUILLAN Gaelic: "cub." Var. and dim: Quill, Quillon.

QUIMBY Old Norse: "from the woman's estate."

QUINCY Latin: "from the fifth son's estate." Dim: Quinn.

QUINLAN Gaelic: "strong; well-informed." Dim: Quinn.

QUINN Gaelic: "wise."

R

RAD Old English: "counselor."

RADBERT Old English: "wise counselor." Dim: Bert, Bertie, Berty.

RADBURN Old English: "from the red stream." Var. and dim: Burnie, Burny, Rad, Radborne, Radbourne.

RADCLIFFE Old English: "from the red cliffs." Dim: Rad, Cliff.

RADFORD Old English: "from the red ford." Var. and dim: Rad, Radferd, Redford.

RADLEY Old English: "from the red meadow." Var. and dim: Lee, Leigh, Rad, Radleigh, Ridley.

RADNOR Old English: "of the red shore." Dim: Rad.

RAFAEL See *Raphael*.

RAFFERTY Gaelic: "prosperous." Dim: Rafe, Raff.

RAFI Arabic: "exalting."

RAHMAN Arabic: "compassionate."

RAINER Teutonic: "mighty army." Var. and dim: Ragnar, Ray, Raynor.

RALEIGH Old English: "of the deer meadow." Var. and dim: Lee, Leigh, Rawley.

RALPH See *Randolph*.

RALSTON Old English: "of Ralph's estate." Dim: Tony.

RAMÓN See *Raymond*.

RAMSDEN Old English: "of the ram valley."

RAMSEY Old English: "ram's island." Var. and dim: Ram, Ramsay.

RANDALL See *Randolph*.

RANDOLPH Old English: "wolf counselor." Var. and dim: Dolf, Dolph, Rafe, Raff, Ralf, Ralph, Ralphie, Rand, Randal, Randall, Randell, Randolf, Randy, Raoul, Rolf, Rolfe, Rolph.

RANGER Old French: "forest guardian." Var: Rainger.

RANON Hebrew: "to sing." Var: Ranen.

RANSOM Old English: "son of the shield."

RAOUL, RAUL See *Randolph; Rudolph*.

RAPHAEL Hebrew: "God has healed." Var. and dim: Rafael, Rafaelle, Rafaello, Rafe, Raff, Raffaello, Ray.

RAVID Hebrew: "ornament."

RAVIV Hebrew: "dew."

RAWDON Teutonic: "from the deer hill." Var: Rawden.

RAY See *Raymond; Roy*.

RAYBURN Old English: "from the deer brook." Var. and dim: Bernie, Burnie, Raeburn, Raybourne, Reyburn.

RAYMOND Teutonic: "wise protector." Var. and dim: Raimondo, Raimund, Raimundo, Ramón, Ray, Raymund, Reamonn.

REDFORD See *Radford*.

REDMOND Teutonic: "adviser; counselor." Var: Radmund, Redman, Redmund.

REECE Old Welsh: "ardent." Var: Rees, Reese, Rhys, Rice.

REED Old English: "red-haired." Var: Read, Reade, Reid.

REEVE Middle English: "steward." Var: Reave, Reeves.

REGAN Gaelic: "little king." Var: Reagan, Reagen, Regen.

REGINALD Teutonic: "mighty ruler." Var. and dim: Raynold, Reg, Reggie, Reggy, Reginauld, Reinald, Reinaldo, Reinaldos, Reinhold, Reinold, Reinwald, Renald, Renaldo, Renato, Renault, René, Rennie, Reynold, Reynolds, Rinaldo, Ron, Ronald, Ronnie, Ronny.

REINHOLD. See *Reginald*.

REMINGTON Old English: "from the raven's estate." Dim: Tony.

REMUS Latin: "swift oarsman."

RENÉ French: "reborn."

RENFRED Teutonic: "peacemaker." Dim: Fred, Freddie, Freddy.

RENSHAW Old English: "from the raven forest." Dim: Rennie, Shaw.

RENWICK Teutonic: "from the raven's nest." Dim: Rennie.

REUBEN Hebrew: "behold, a son." Var. and dim: Reuven, Rouvin, Rube, Ruben, Rubin, Ruby.

REX Latin: "king."

REXFORD Old English: "of the king's ford." Dim: Rex, Ford.

REYNARD Teutonic: "mighty." Old French: "fox." Var. and dim: Ray, Raynard, Reinhard, Rennard, Renaud, Rey.

REYNOLD See *Reginald*.

RICHARD Teutonic: "powerful; valiant." Var. and dim: Dick, Dicky, Ric, Ricard, Ricardo, Riccardo, Rich, Richart, Richie, Richy, Rick, Rickert, Ricki, Rickie, Ricky, Rico, Riki, Riocard, Ritchie.

RICHMOND Teutonic: "powerful protector." Dim: Rich, Richie.

RIDA Arabic: "favored."

RIDER Old English: "horseman." Var: Ryder.

RIDGE Old English: "from the ridge."

RIDGELEY Old English: "from the meadow ridge." Dim: Lee, Leigh.

RIDGEWAY Old English: "from the ridge road." Dim: Ridge.

RILEY Gaelic: "valiant one." Var: Reilly, Ryley.

RING Old English: "ring." Dim: Ringo.

RINGO Japanese: "apple."

RIORDAN Gaelic: "bard; royal poet." Dim: Dan, Danny.

RIP See *Ripley; Robert*.

RIPLEY Old English: "from the shouter's meadow." Var. and dim: Lee, Leigh, Rip, Ripleigh.

ROALD Teutonic: "famous ruler."

ROARKE Gaelic: "famous ruler." Var: Rourke.

ROBERT Old English: "bright fame." Var. and dim: Bert, Bertie, Berty, Bob, Bobbie, Bobby, Rab,

Riobard, Rip, Rob, Robb, Robbie, Robby, Roberto, Robin, Rupert, Ruperto, Ruprecht.

ROBERTSON Old English: "son of Robert." (Also see *Robert*.)

ROBIN See *Robert*.

ROBINSON Old English: "son of Robert; son of Robin." (Also see *Robert*.)

ROCHESTER Old English: "from the rocky fort." Dim: Ches, Chester, Rock, Rockie, Rocky.

ROCKWELL Old English: "from the rocky spring." Dim: Rock, Rockie, Rocky.

RODERICK Teutonic: "famous ruler." Var. and dim: Rick, Rickie, Ricky, Rod, Rodd, Roddie, Roddy, Roderic, Roderich, Roderigo, Rodrigo, Rodrique, Rory.

RODGER See *Roger*.

RODMAN Teutonic: "famous man." Dim: Manny, Rod, Rodd, Roddie, Roddy.

RODNEY Old English: "from the island clearing." Dim: Rod, Rodd, Roddie, Roddy.

ROGER Teutonic: "famous spearman." Var. and dim: Rodge, Rodger, Rodgers, Rog, Rogerio, Rogers, Rory, Rüdiger, Ruggiero, Rutger.

ROLAND Teutonic: "from the famous land." Var. and dim: Lannie, Lanny, Orland, Orlando, Rolando, Rollie, Rollin, Rollins, Rollo, Rolly, Rowe, Rowland.

ROLF See *Randolph*; *Rudolph*.

ROMAN Latin: "from Rome." Var: Romain.

ROMEO Latin: "pilgrim to Rome."

ROMNEY Welsh: "curving river."

ROMULUS Latin: "citizen of Rome."

RONALD See *Reginald*.

RONEL Hebrew: "joy of God." Dim: Ronnie, Ronny.

ROONEY Gaelic: "red-haired." Var: Rowan, Rowe, Rowen.

ROPER Old English: "ropemaker."

RORY See *Roderick*; *Roger*.

ROSCOE Teutonic: "from the deer forest." Dim: Ross, Rossie, Rossy.

ROSS Old French: "red." Teutonic: "horse." Gaelic: "of the headlands." Dim: Rossie, Rossy.

ROSWELL Teutonic: "mighty steed." Var: Roswald.

ROTH Teutonic: "red-haired."

ROWAN, ROWEN See *Rooney*.

ROY French: "king." Celtic: "red-haired." Var: Rey, Roi. (Also see *Leroy*.)

ROYAL French: "royal." Dim: Roy.

ROYCE Old English: "son of the king." Dim: Roy.

ROYD Old Norse: "from the forest clearing."

ROYDEN Old English: "from the king's hill." Var. and dim: Roy, Roydon.

RUDOLPH Teutonic: "famous wolf." Var. and dim: Dolf, Dolph, Raoul, Raul, Rodolfo, Rodolph, Rodolphe, Rolf, Rolfe, Rollo, Rolph, Rudie, Rudolf, Rudolfo, Rudy.

RUDY See *Rudolph*; *Rudyard*.

RUDYARD Old English: "from the red enclosure." Dim: Rudy.

RUFORD Old English: "from the red ford." Var: Rufford.

RUFUS Latin: "red-haired." Dim: Rufe.

RUNAKO Zezuru/Zimbabwe: "handsome."

RUPERT See *Robert*.

RUSKIN Old French: "red-haired." Dim: Russ.

RUSSELL   Old French: "red-haired." Dim: Russ, Rusty.

RUTHERFORD   Old English: "from the cattle crossing." Dim: Ford.

RUTLEDGE   Old English: "from the red pool."

RUTLEY   Old English: "from the root meadow." Dim: Lee, Leigh.

RWIZI   Zezuru/Zimbabwe: "of the river."

RYAN   Gaelic: "little king."

RYCROFT   Old English: "from the rye field."

RYLAN   Old English: "from the rye land." Var: Ryland.

SABIN Latin: "man of the Sabine people."

SADIKI Swahili/East Africa: "faithful."

SAFFORD Old English: "of the willow ford." Dim: Ford.

SAL See *Salisbury; Salvatore*.

SALISBURY Old English: "from the strong hold." Dim: Sal.

SALVATORE Italian: "savior." Var. and dim: Sal, Sallie, Sally, Salvador, Sauveur.

SAM See *Samson; Samuel*.

SAMSON Hebrew: "like the sun." Var. and dim: Sam, Sammie, Sammy, Sampson, Sansom, Sansón, Sansone, Shimshon, Sonnie, Sonny.

SAMUEL Hebrew: "God has heard." Var. and dim: Sam, Sammie, Sammy, Samuele.

SANBORN Old English: "from the sandy brook." Var. and dim: Sandborn, Sandy.

SANCHO Latin: "sanctified."

SANDER, SANDOR See *Alexander*.

SANDERS Middle English: "son of Alexander." (Also see *Alexander*.)

SANFORD Old English: "from the sandy crossing." Dim: Sandy.

SARGENT Old French: "military attendant." Var. and dim: Sarge, Sargeant, Sergent.

SAUL Hebrew: "longed for." Var. and dim: Sol, Sollie, Solly.

SAVILLE Old French: "from the willow estate." Var: Savill.

SAWYER Middle English: "sawer of wood." (Also see *Sayer*.)

SAXON Old English: "Saxon; swordsman."

SAYER Welsh: "carpenter." Var: Sayers, Sayre, Sayres.

SCHUYLER Dutch: "scholar." Dim: Sky.

SCOTT Old English: "native of Scotland." Var. and dim: Scot, Scottie, Scotty.

SEABROOK Old English: "from the seaside brook." Var. and dim: Brook, Seaborn, Seabrooke.

SEADON Old English: "from the hill by the sea." Dim: Don, Donny.

SEALY Old English: "blessed; happy." Var: Seeley, Seelye.

SEAMUS See *James*.

SEAN See *John*.

SEARLE Teutonic: "armed." Var: Serle.

SEATON Old English: "from the seaside town." Var. and dim: Seton, Tony.

SEBASTIAN Greek: "venerated; majestic." Var: Sebastiano, Sébastien.

SEDGEWICK Old English: "victorious town." Var. and dim: Sedge, Sedgwick, Sedgewinn.

SELBY Old English: "from the manor farm."

SELDON Old English: "from the manor valley." Var. and dim: Don, Donnie, Donny, Selden.

SELIG Teutonic: "blessed." Var: Zelig.

SELWYN Anglo-Saxon: "friend at court." Var. and dim: Selwin, Winnie, Winny, Wynn.

SERGIO Italian: "attendant." Var: Serge.

SETH Hebrew: "appointed."

SEUMAS See *James*.

SEWARD Old English: "sea guardian."

SEWELL Teutonic: "victorious at sea." Var: Sewald, Sewall.

SEYMOUR Teutonic: "famed at sea." Var. and dim: Morey, Morrie, Morry, Seymore.

SHADWELL Old English: "from the arbor spring." Dim: Shad.

SHAI Hebrew: "gift."

SHAMIR Hebrew: "strong."

SHAMUS See *James*.

SHANNON Gaelic: "little wise one."

SHARIF Arabic: "honest."

SHAW Old English: "from the grove."

SHAWN See *John*.

SHEEHAN Gaelic: "little peaceful one."

SHEFFIELD Old English: "from the crooked field." Dim: Sheff.

SHELBY Old English: "from the farm on the ledge." Dim: Shelley, Shelly.

SHELDON Old English: "from the hut on the hill." Var. and dim: Shelley, Shelly, Shelton, Skelton.

SHELLEY Old English: "from the ledge meadow." Var: Shelly. (Also see *Shelby; Sheldon*.)

SHEPHERD Old English: "shepherd." Var. and dim: Shep, Shepard, Shepp, Sheppard, Shepperd.

SHEPLEY Old English: "of the sheep meadow." Dim: Shep, Lee, Leigh.

SHERBORNE Old English: "from the clear brook." Var: Sherborn, Sherbourne, Sherburne.

SHERIDAN Gaelic: "wild man." Dim: Dan, Dannie, Danny.

SHERLOCK Old English: "fair-haired."

SHERMAN Anglo-Saxon: "one who shears." Dim: Mannie, Manny, Sherm.

SHERWIN Old English: "shining friend." Dim: Win, Winnie, Winny.

SHERWOOD Old English: "of the bright forest." Dim: Woodie, Woody.

SHONARI Swahili/East Africa: "strong."

SHUMBA Zezuru/Zimbabwe: "lion."

SIDNEY Old French: "St. Dennis." Also from Sidon, the city in Phoenicia. Var. and dim: Sid, Syd, Sydney.

SIEGFRIED Teutonic: "victorious peace." Var. and dim: Sig, Sigfrid, Siggy, Sigvard.

SIGMUND Teutonic: "victorious protector." Var. and dim: Sig, Siggy, Sigismond, Sigismund, Sigmond.

SILAS See *Silvanus*.

SILVANUS Latin: "god of the woodlands; man of the forest." Var: Silas, Silvain, Silvan, Silvano, Silvio, Sylvan.

SILVESTER See *Sylvester*.

SIMCHA Hebrew: "joy." (Also used as a girl's name.)

SIMON Hebrew: "to be heard." Var. and dim: Si, Sim, Simeon.

SIMPSON Old English: "son of Simon." Var. and dim: Sim, Simson, Sonnie, Sonny.

SINCLAIR Latin: "shining." Old French: "St. Clair."

SIVAN Hebrew: the ninth month of the Hebrew calendar.

SIYOLO Xhosa/South Africa: "joyful."

SKELLY Gaelic: "storyteller." Var: Skelley.

SKIP Old Norse: "ship owner." Var. and dim: Skipper, Skippie, Skippy.

SLADE Old English: "valley dweller."

SLOAN Gaelic: "warrior." Var: Sloane. (Also used as a girl's name.)

SOL Latin: "sun." (Also see *Saul; Solomon*.)

SOLOMON Hebrew: "peace." Var. and dim: Salmon, Salomon, Shalom, Sholom, Sol, Sollie, Solly.

SOLON Greek: "wise man."

SOMERSET Old English: "of the summer settlers."

SOMERVILLE Old English: "from the summer estate."

SPALDING Old English: "from the divided meadow." Var: Spaulding.

SPENCER Middle English: "steward; guardian." Var. and dim: Spence, Spenser.

SPRAGUE Teutonic: "lively."

STACEY Latin: "prosperous; established." Var: Stacy.

STAFFORD Old English: "from the landing ford." Dim: Ford.

STANBURY Old English: "from the stone fortress." Dim: Stan.

STANDISH Old English: "from the stony park." Dim: Stan.

STANFIELD Old English: "from the rocky field." Dim: Field, Stan.

STANFORD Old English: "from the stony ford." Var. and dim: Stamford, Stan.

STANHOPE Old English: "from the rocky hollow." Dim: Stan.

STANISLAUS Polish: "glory of the camp." Var. and dim: Stan, Stanislas.

STANLEY Old English: "of the rocky meadow." Var. and dim: Lee, Leigh, Stan, Stanleigh.

STANTON Old English: "from the stony farm." Dim: Stan, Tony.

STANWAY Old English: "dweller on the stone road." Dim: Stan.

STANWICK Old English: "from the rocky village." Dim: Stan, Wick.

STANWOOD Old English: "from the stony wood." Dim: Stan, Woodie, Woody.

STEDMAN Old English: "dweller at the farmstead." Var: Steadman.

STEFAN See *Stephen*.

STEPHEN Greek: "crown." Var. and dim: Étienne, Esteban, Estevan, Stefan, Stefano, Steffen, Stephan, Stephanus, Stevan, Steve, Steven, Stevie.

STERLING Old English: "of excellent quality." Var: Stirling.

STEVEN See *Stephen*.

STEWART Old English: "steward; administrator." Var. and dim: Steward, Stu, Stuart.

STILLMAN Old English: "quiet man." Dim: Mannie, Manny.

STILWELL Anglo-Saxon: "from the quiet spring."

STODDARD Old English: "keeper of horses."

STROUD Old English: "of the thicket."

STRUTHERS Gaelic: "of the stream."

STUART See *Stewart*.

SUDI Swahili: "lucky."

SUFFIELD Old English: "from the south field." Dim: Field.

SULLIVAN Gaelic: "black-eyed."

SUMNER Latin: "summoner; church official." Var: Summner.

SUTCLIFF Old English: "from the south cliff." Var. and dim: Cliff, Sutcliffe.

SUTHERLAND Old Norse: "from the southern land."

SUTTON Old English: "from the south town."

SVEN Old Norse: "youth." Var: Svend, Swain, Swaine.

SWEENEY Gaelic: "little hero."

SYDNEY See *Sidney*.

SYLVESTER Latin: "of the woods." Var: Silvester. (Also see *Silvanus*.)

T

TAB Middle English: "drummer." Var. and dim: Tabbie, Tabby, Taber, Tabor.

TAD See *Thaddeus*.

TAHIR Arabic: "pure."

TALBOT Teutonic: "valley-bright." Old English: "bloodhound." Var. and dim: Talbert, Talbott, Tallie, Tally.

TAM, TAMMIE, TAMMY See *Thomas*.

TAMIR Hebrew: "tall." Var: Timur.

TATE Teutonic: "cheerful." Var: Tait.

TANNER Old English: "leather worker." Dim: Tannie, Tanny.

TARLETON Old English: "Thor's town." Dim: Tony.

TAYLOR Middle English: "tailor." Var: Tailor.

TEAGUE Gaelic: "poet; bard."

TEARLE Old English: "stern one."

TED See *Edward; Theobald; Theodore; Theodoric.*

TELFORD Old French: "ironworker." Var. and dim: Ford, Telfer, Telfor, Telfour.

TEMPLETON Old English: "temple town." Dim: Temple, Tony.

TENNESSEE for the American state.

TENNYSON Middle English: "son of Dennis."

TERENCE Latin: "tender; gracious." Var. and dim: Terrence, Terry.

TERRELL Old English: "like Thor." Var: Terrill, Tirrell.

TERRY See *Terence*.

TERTIUS Latin: "third (child)."

THADDEUS Latin: "praiser." Var. and dim: Tad, Tadd, Taddeo, Tadeo, Thad.

THATCHER Old English: "thatcher; roofer." Var. and dim: Thacher, Thackeray, Thatch, Thaxter.

THAYER Teutonic: "of the nation's army."

THEMBA Xhosa/South Africa: "hope."

THEOBALD Teutonic: "people's prince." Var. and dim: Ted, Teddie, Teddy, Thebault, Theo, Thibaud, Thibaut, Tibold, Tybald, Tybalt.

THEODORE Greek: "gift of God." Var. and dim: Ted, Teddie, Teddy, Teodor, Teodore, Theo, Theodor, Tudor.

THEODORIC Teutonic: "ruler of the people." Var. and dim: Derek, Derrick, Dieter, Dietrich, Dirk, Ted, Teddie, Teddy, Theo.

THERON Greek: "hunter." Var: Theran, Therron.

THOMAS Hebrew-Aramaic: "twin." Var. and dim: Tam, Tamas, Tammie, Tammy, Tavis, Tavish, Thom, Tom, Tomás, Tomaso, Tommie, Tommy.

THOR Old Norse: "thunder." Var: Tor.

THORBERT Old Norse: "Thor's brilliance." Var: Torbert.

THORLEY Old English: "Thor's meadow." Var: Torley.

THORNDIKE Old English: "from the thorny embankment." Var. and dim: Thorn, Thorndyke.

THORNTON Old English: "from the thorn tree farm." Dim: Thorn, Tony.

THORPE Old English: "from the village." Var: Thorp.

THURMAN Scandinavian: "under Thor's protection." Var: Thurmond.

THURSTON Scandinavian: "Thor's stone." Var: Thorsten, Thurstan.

TIERNEY Gaelic: "lordly one." Var: Tiernan.

TILDEN Old English: "from the liberal one's valley."

TILFORD Old English: "from the liberal one's ford."

TILTON Old English: "from the liberal one's estate."

TIM See *Timothy*.

TIMOTHY Greek: "honoring God." Var. and dim: Tim, Timmie, Timmy, Timoteo, Timothée, Timotheus, Tymon.

TITUS Greek: "of the giants." Var: Tito.

TIVON Hebrew: "nature lover."

TOBIAS Hebrew: "God is good." Var. and dim: Tobe, Tobiah, Tobie, Tobin, Tobit, Toby.

TODD Norse: "fox." Var. and dim: Todd, Toddie, Toddy.

TOLAND Old English: "of the taxed land." Var: Tolland, Towland.

TOM See *Thomas*.

TONY See *Anthony*.

TORRANCE Gaelic: "of the knolls." Var. and dim: Torey, Torrence, Torrey, Torry.

TOWNLEY Old English: "from the town meadow." Dim: Lee.

TOWNSEND Old English: "from the town's end."

TRACEY Anglo-Saxon: "brave one." Var. and dim: Trace, Tracy.

TRAHERN Old Welsh: "strong as iron."

TRAVIS Old French: "from the crossroads." Var: Travers.

TREMAYNE Celtic: "from the stony town." Var: Tremain.

TRENT Latin: "swift."

TREVOR Gaelic: "prudent."

TRISTAN Celtic: "bold." Old French: "sorrowful." Var. and dim: Tris, Tristram.

TROY for the ancient city.

TRUMAN Old English: "faithful man." Var: Trueman.

TUCKER Old English: "fuller or tucker of cloth." Dim: Tuck.

TUDOR See *Theodore*.

TURNER Latin: "worker with the lathe."

TYLER Old English: "worker with tiles." Dim: Ty.

TYRONE Greek: "sovereign." Dim: Ty.

TYSON Teutonic: "son of the German." Dim: Sonnie, Sonny, Ty.

U

UDELL Old English: "from the yew tree valley."
Var. and dim: Dell, Udale, Udall.

UDO Igbo/Nigeria: "peace."

UGO Igbo/Nigeria: "eagle."

UHURU Kenya: "freedom."

ULAND Teutonic: "of the noble land."

ULMER Old Norse: "wolf fame."

ULRICH Teutonic: "wolf ruler." Var. and dim: Rick,
Rickie, Ricky, Ulric, Ulrick.

ULYSSES Greek: "wrathful."

UMI Malawi: "life."

UPTON Old English: "from the upper town." Dim:
Tony.

URBAN Latin: "town dweller; courteous." Var:
Urbain, Urbano, Urbanus.

URI Hebrew: "my light."

URIAH Hebrew: "God is my light." Var: Uriel.

V

VACHEL French: "keeper of cattle."

VAIL Middle English: "from the valley." Var: Vale.

VAL See *Valentine*.

VALDIS Teutonic: "spirited in battle." Dim: Val.

VALENTINE Latin: "healthy." Var. and dim: Val,
Valentin, Valentino.

VAN Dutch: "from; of." (A common diminutive for
Dutch surnames beginning with Van.)

VANCE Middle English: "thresher."

Van NESS Dutch: "from the headlands." Dim: Van.

Van WYCK Dutch: "from the refuge." Dim: Van.

VARDEN Old French: "from the green hill." Var:
Vardon.

VARIAN Latin: "changeable; capricious."

VARNEY Celtic: "from the alder grove."

VAUGHN Welsh: "small." Var: Vaughan.

VERNON Latin: "springlike; youthful." Dim: Vern,
Verne.

VICTOR Latin: "conqueror." Var. and dim: Vic, Vick, Vittorio.

VINCENT Latin: "conquering." Dim: Vin, Vince, Vinnie, Vinny.

VINSON Old English: "son of Vincent." Dim: Sonny, Vin, Vince, Vinnie, Vinny.

VINTON Old English: "wine town." Dim: Tony, Vin, Vinnie, Vinny.

VIRGIL Latin: "staff bearer: flourishing." Var. and dim: Verge, Vergil, Virge, Virgilio.

VITO Latin: "vital; alive."

VLADIMIR Slavic: "powerful ruler." Dim: Vlad.

VOLNEY Teutonic: "spirit of the people."

W

WADE Old English: "wanderer; dweller at the river crossing."

WADSWORTH Old English: "from Wade's estate." Var: Wadesworth.

WAINWRIGHT Old English: "wagonmaker." Dim: Wayne, Wright.

WAITE Middle English: "watchman."

WAKEFIELD Old English: "from the wet field."

WALCOTT Old English: "from the walled cottage."

WALDEMAR Teutonic: "strong and famous." Var. and dim: Valdemar, Waldo, Wallie, Wally.

WALDEN Old English: "from the wooded valley." Dim: Wallie, Wally.

WALDO See *Oswald; Waldemar.*

WALDRON Teutonic: "mighty raven."

WALFORD Old English: "from the Welshman's crossing." Dim: Wallie, Wally.

WALKER Old English: "thickener of cloth; fuller."

WALLACE Old English: "Welshman." Teutonic: "foreigner." Var. and dim: Wallache, Wallas, Wallie, Wallis, Wally, Walsh, Welch, Welsh.

WALSTON Anglo-Saxon: "cornerstone." Dim: Tony.

WALTER Teutonic: "powerful warrior." Var. and dim: Gauthier, Gautier, Gualterio, Gualtiero, Wallie, Wally, Walt, Walther.

WALTON Old English: "from the walled town." Dim: Tony, Wallie, Wally, Walt.

WARD Old English: "watchman; guardian." Var: Warden, Worden.

WARE Old English: "prudent."

WARFIELD Old English: "from the field by the dam."

WARFORD Old English: "from the ford by the dam." Dim: Ford.

WARLEY Old English: "from the meadow by the dam." Dim: Lee, Leigh.

WARNER Teutonic: "armed defender." Var: Werner, Wernher.

WARREN Teutonic: "defender." Middle English: "game warden." Var: Waring.

WARRICK Teutonic: "defending ruler." Old English: "stronghold." Var: Warwick.

WARTON Old English: "from the town by the dam." Dim: Tony.

WASHBURN Old English: "from the flooding brook." Dim: Bernie, Burnie, Burny.

WASHINGTON Old English: "from the keen one's estate."

WATSON Old English: "son of Walter." Dim: Sonnie, Sonny.

WAVERLY Old English: "of the trembling aspen meadow." Dim: Lee, Leigh.

WAYLAND Old English: "from the land near the highway."

WAYNE See *Wainwright*.

WEBB Old English: "weaver." Var: Weber, Webster.

WELBY Old English: "from the spring farm."

WELDON Old English: "from the spring by the hill."

WELFORD Old English: "from the spring by the crossing."

WELLINGTON Old English: "from the wealthy one's estate."

WELLS Old English: "from the spring."

WENDELL Teutonic: "wanderer." Var: Wendel.

WERNER See *Warner*.

WESLEY Old English: "from the west meadow." Var. and dim: Lee, Leigh, Wes, Westleigh, Westley.

WESTBROOK Old English: "from the west brook." Var. and dim: Brook, Brooke, Wes, West, Westbrooke.

WESTON Old English: "from the western estate." Dim: Tony, Wes, West.

WETHERBY Old English: "from the wethersheep farm."

WETHERLY Old English: "from the wethersheep meadow." Dim: Lee, Leigh.

WEYLIN Celtic: "son of the wolf."

WHARTON Old English: "from the estate in the hollow."

WHEATLEY Old English: "of the wheat meadow." Var. and dim: Lee, Leigh, Wheatly.

WHEATON Old English: "from the wheat estate." Dim: Tony.

WHEELER Old English: "wheelmaker."

WHITBY Old English: "from the white farmstead."

WHITCOMB Old English: "from the white hollow." Dim: Whit.

WHITELAW Old English: "from the white hill."

WHITFIELD Old English: "from the white field." Dim: Whit, Field.

WHITFORD Old English: "from the white, or clear, ford." Dim: Whit, Ford.

WHITLEY Old English: "from the white meadow." Dim: Lee, Leigh, Whit.

WHITMAN Old English: "white-haired, or fair-haired, man." Dim: Whit.

WHITNEY Old English: "from the white island."

WHITTAKER Old English: "dweller at the white field." Dim: Whit.

WHICKHAM Old English: "from the village enclosure." Dim: Wick.

WICKLEY Old English: "from the village meadow." Dim: Lee, Leigh, Wick.

WILBUR See *Gilbert*.

WILEY See *William*.

WILFRED Teutonic: "peaceful resolve." Var. and dim: Wilfrid, Will, Willie, Willy.

WILHELM See *William*.

WILLARD Teutonic: "brave; resolute." Dim: Will, Willie, Willy.

WILLIAM Teutonic: "resolute guardian." Var. and dim: Bill, Billie, Billy, Guglielmo, Guillaume, Guillermo, Liam, Wiley, Wilkes, Wilkie, Wilhelm, Will, Willem, Willi, Willie, Willis, Willy.

WILLOUGHBY Teutonic: "from the place by the willows." Dim: Will, Willie, Willy.

WILMER Teutonic: "famous; resolute." Var. and dim: Will, Willie, Willy, Wilmar.

WILMOT Teutonic: "resolute spirit." Dim: Will, Willie, Willy.

WILSON Old English: "son of William." Dim: Sonny, Will, Willie, Willy.

WILTON Old English: "from the spring farm." Dim: Tony, Will, Willie, Willy.

WINCHELL Old English: "from the bend in the road." Dim: Win, Winnie, Winny.

WINDSOR Old English: "from the river's bend."

WINFIELD Old English: "from the friendly field." Dim: Win, Winnie, Winny.

WINFRED Old English: "peaceful friend." Var. and dim: Fred, Win, Winfrid, Winnie, Winny.

WINSLOW Old English: "from the friend's hill." Dim: Win, Winnie, Winny.

WINSTON Old English: "from the friendly town." Dim: Tony, Win, Winnie, Winny.

WINTHROP Old English: "from the friendly village." Dim: Win, Winnie, Winny.

WINWARD Old English: "friend and guardian." Dim: Win, Winnie, Winny.

WOLCOTT Old English: "from Wolfe's cottage." Var: Woolcott.

WOLFE Teutonic: "wolf." Var: Wolf.

WOLFGANG Teutonic: "path of the wolf." Dim: Wolf, Wolfe.

WOLFRAM Teutonic: "wolf raven."

WOODLEY Old English: "from the wooded meadow." Dim: Lee, Leigh.

WOODROW Old English: "from the hedgerow by the forest." Dim: Woodie, Woody.

WOODWARD Old English: "forest warden." Dim: Ward, Woodie, Woody.

WOODY See *Woodrow, Woodward*.

WORTH Old English: "of the farmstead."

WORTHINGTON Anglo-Saxon: "from the river's edge." Dim: Tony.

WRIGHT Old English: "craftsman."

WYATT French: "guide." Var. and dim: Wiatt, Wye.

WYCLIFF Old English: "from the white cliffs." Dim: Cliff.

WYLIE Old English: "charming." (Also see *William*.)

WYMAN Old English: "warrior." Dim: Mannie, Manny.

WYMER Old English: "famous in battle."

WYNDHAM Old English: "from the winding village."

WYNN Old Welsh: "fair one." Var: Winn.

WYSTAN Anglo-Saxon: "battle stone." Dim: Stan.

WYTHE Middle English: "dweller by the willows."

X

XANTHUS   Greek: "golden-haired."
XAVIER   Arabic: "bright." Var: Javier, Xever.
XENOS   Greek: "stranger."
XERXES   Persian: "king."
XIMENES   a Spanish form of *Simon*.
XYLON   Greek: "from the forest."

Y

YADID Hebrew: "friend."

YALE Teutonic: "who pays or yields." Old English: "from the corner of the land."

YAMURO Zezuru/Zimbabwe: "helper."

YANCY French corruption of the word for "Englishman." Var: Yancey, Yankee.

YARDLEY Old English: "from the enclosed meadow." Dim: Lee, Leigh.

YATES Old English: "dweller at the gates." Var: Yeats.

YAVNIEL Hebrew: "God will build."

YEHUDI See *Judah*.

YIGAL Hebrew: "He will redeem."

YOAV Hebrew: "God is the father."

YORAM Hebrew: "God is exalted."

YORK Celtic: "yew tree."

YULE Anglo-Saxon: "born at Christmas." Var: Yul.

YURI See *George*.

YVES See *Ivar*.

ZACHARY Hebrew: "God hath remembered." Var. and dim: Zacarias, Zaccaria, Zach, Zachariah, Zacharias, Zacharie, Zak, Zakarias, Zechariah, Zeke.

ZAMIR Hebrew: "songbird."

ZANE See *John*.

ZEBADIAH Hebrew: "gift of the Lord." Dim. Zeb.

ZEBULON Hebrew: "dwelling place." Dim: Zeb.

ZEDEKIAH Hebrew: "God is righteousness." Dim: Zed.

ZEKE See *Ezekiel; Zachary*.

ZELIG See *Selig*.

ZERACH Hebrew: "rising light."

ZEVI Hebrew: "deer." Var: Zev, Zvi.

ZOLA Xhosa/South Africa: "peaceful."

ZUBERI Swahili/East Africa: "strong."

AMERICA'S MOST POPULAR NAMES

As has been said in the introduction to this book, national, ethnic, religious and family traditions play their parts in the naming of children. The fads and fashions of the day, particularly in relation to girls' names, exert strong influences as well, as can be seen in the lists that follow.

America is a large country, and a great melting pot of people from every national, racial and religious background, so perhaps the best sampling of America's most popular names is from the birth records of its great melting-pot city, New York City.

The first listings show how the ten most popular girls' and boys' names changed over a period of fifty years, from 1898 to 1948. Following that are listings of the most popular names for each of the five years from 1984 through 1988.

Notice how the names with the highest ratings tend to have the greatest staying power, how the names near the center of the lists move up and down, seeming to vie for position, and how new names slowly find their way onto the top-ten lists.

		1898	1928	1948
	1	Mary	Mary	Linda
	2	Catherine	Marie	Mary
	3	Margaret	Annie	Barbara
G	4	Annie	Margaret	Patricia
I	5	Rose	Catherine	Susan
R	6	Marie	Gloria	Kathleen
L	7	Esther	Helen	Carol
S	8	Sarah	Teresa	Nancy
	9	Frances	Joan	Margaret
	10	Ida	Barbara	Diane
	1	John	John	Robert
	2	William	William	John
	3	Charles	Joseph	James
B	4	George	James	Michael
O	5	Joseph	Richard	William
Y	6	Edward	Edward	Richard
S	7	James	Robert	Joseph
	8	Louis	Thomas	Thomas
	9	Francis	George	Stephen
	10	Samuel	Louis	David

	1984	1985	1986	1987	1988
1	Jennifer	Jennifer	Jessica	Jessica	Jessica
2	Jessica	Jessica	Jennifer	Jennifer	Jennifer
G 3	Melissa	Christina	Stephanie	Stephanie	Stephanie
I 4	Stephanie	Stephanie	Nicole	Melissa	Melissa
R 5	Nicole	Melissa	Christina	Christina	Nicole
L 6	Christina	Nicole	Amanda	Nicole	Ashley
S 7	Tiffany	Elizabeth	Melissa	Amanda	Tiffany
8	Danielle	Amanda	Tiffany	Ashley	Amanda
9	Elizabeth	Danielle	Danielle*	Tiffany	Christina
10	Lauren	Lauren	Elizabeth*	Samantha	Samantha

		Michael	Michael	Michael	Michael
	1	Michael	Christopher	Christopher	Christopher
	2	Christopher	Daniel	Jonathan	Jonathan
B	3	Daniel	David	Anthony	Daniel
O	4	David	Anthony	David	Daniel
Y	5	Joseph	Joseph	Daniel	David
S	6	Anthony	Jonathan	Joseph	Anthony
	7	Jason	Jason	John	Joseph
	8	Jonathan	John	Jason	Matthew
	9	John	Robert	Andrew	John
	10	Robert			Andrew

		Michael
	1	Michael
	2	Christopher
	3	Jonathan
	4	Daniel
	5	Anthony
	6	David
	7	Joseph
	8	Matthew
	9	John
	10	Andrew

*Tied